Study Guide

for

Mynatt and Doherty

Understanding Human Behavior

Second Edition

prepared by

Kathy Hipp
Bowling Green University

Allyn and Bacon
Boston   London   Toronto   Sydney   Tokyo   Singapore

ISBN 0-205-33467-9

Printed in the United States of America

10 9 8 7 6 5 4 3 2 1   04 03 02 01

Table of Contents

Introduction

This study guide was prepared to accompany the second edition of *Understanding Human Behavior*, by Clifford R. Mynatt and Michael E. Doherty. The main goal in writing any study guide is to assist students in learning, understanding, and remembering the material covered in the text. A good deal of the material from the study guide accompanying the first edition of this text was retained for the second edition, and the credit for the first edition goes to Linda Skinner of Middle Tennessee State University.

If you haven't skimmed through your textbook yet, you should do so now. You'll see that the authors have organized it very differently from the way most General Psychology textbooks are organized. If you read the Introduction and the "How to Study -- Especially This Book" sections, you'll see that the authors intentionally titled each chapter with well-founded conclusions about human behavior that are communicated in an "everyday language" kind of way. Even the headings and subheadings within each chapter are straightforward, and within the chapter is where you'll find the evidence to support each of the assertions in the chapter titles. One of the reasons the authors did this is to give you a way to form an outline for each chapter as you're learning the material. One of the things you'll discover in this course is that learning and retention are *greatly* enhanced when the material is being incorporated into an already-existing framework (we call these frameworks "schemas," and you'll learn more about them in chapter 19, "The More You Know, the Easier It Is to Learn New Things"). Equally important is that the framework come from within you, which is why learning is much easier when you *actively* create your framework to incorporate new facts and ideas, rather than passively sit back and stare at a pre-existing outline.

In my opinion, the best advice you can get for understanding this material and doing well in this course is exactly what the authors describe in the Introduction and "How to Study" sections. Both of the authors were my advisors in graduate school at Bowling Green State University, so believe me when I say they know what they are talking about when it comes to teaching and understanding psychology. There are just a few things I would like to highlight from my own experience throughout college and graduate school, both as a student and as an instructor.

(1) Do not simply go through your text with a highlighter. Remember, learning should be *active,* so you will be much better off with a pen or pencil in hand, whether you're writing in your textbook or taking notes as you read. With a pen rather than a highlighter, you can immediately write down any questions, thoughts, ideas, or ways of putting into your own words the things you're reading about (another fantastic way to help you understand and remember what you're learning).

(2) Try to study with other people whenever possible. Another thing I've found in my experience is that I always understood and remembered material better when I could figure out a way to explain it to someone else. Even if you can't find people to form a study group, you should try to be able to explain everything you're learning about to yourself...and it will help to actually explain it to yourself, out loud.

(3) Back to the active frameworks. The Basic Ideas the authors provide are another great way, along with the chapter titles, to use a framework to guide your learning. I strongly suggest that you write out the list of Basic Ideas (they're all listed in the Introduction) and leave room between them. As you read through the text throughout the semester, use the list to jot down notes about how what you're learning about supports the different Basic Ideas (there is also a place to do this in the study guide, in the last chapter of each of the 12 Parts of the text). Having it all in one place, though, will also allow you to reread what you wrote for previous chapters, which will enhance understanding and retention.

(4) As the authors mention, they have not written summaries for each chapter, but to get an idea of what each chapter is about before you read it (which is another great learning tool), they suggest simply skimming through the chapter itself and reading the headings and subheadings. I would suggest you also do this with the study guide. The first section for each chapter includes key terms, concepts, and questions that serve as a review of the chapter. Getting an idea about what you're preparing to learn is a great way to help you learn and remember the material ahead of you.

(5) Ask questions. Anytime. All the time. In spite of what I would usually like to think, I'm not perfect...so it's remotely possible that the material in this study guide may contain a mistake. If you find something that you think may be wrong, you can only benefit from bringing it to your TA or instructor. If the study guide is correct, you need to know why it's correct so you can change your thinking about the topic in question. If the study guide is wrong, you need affirmation that your understanding is right. Of course, you also should not hesitate to ask your TA or instructor any other questions you have about the material.

Organization of This Study Guide

The main goal of this study guide is to facilitate learning. To that end, four different sections are included for most of the chapters, each with a different purpose.

Checking Your Knowledge: Terms, Statements, & Questions. This section serves to help you review the material in the chapter by defining terms, explaining concepts, and answering questions.

Expanding Your Knowledge and Understanding. This section includes questions and exercises meant to help you understand and use the material from the chapter.

Testing Your Knowledge and Understanding: Multiple Choice Questions. Practice multiple choice questions are included; however, you should understand that they do not cover all of the material for any given chapter. You should not assume that answering them will fully prepare you to take a multiple choice exam in your class. Along the same lines, you should not assume that any other material that is emphasized in a chapter in this study guide (such as in the "Expanding" or "Applying" sections) are the *only* things that are important from that chapter. Your instructor may have very different ideas about what is more and less important, and the study guide could not include exercises for everything.

Applying Your Knowledge and Understanding: Challenge. This section provides you with the opportunity to take the material beyond reading and apply it in various ways. You will be asked to *think* about the material in ways that you may not have thought about it before.

This brings me to the conclusion. One of the things I love about psychology is that I have a much better understanding of the people around me, as well as all sorts of things that happen in the world, because of what I know about psychology. So I encourage you to continuously look around in your day-to-day life to find ways of applying what you learn about in this course. Not only does it make life more interesting and understandable, it will help you remember what you learn...and hopefully ace that final exam. Good luck, and most importantly, enjoy psychology!

Chapter 1 -- Science Works

(or Why People Argue about Politics but Not about Whether the Earth Revolves around the Sun)

Checking Your Knowledge: Terms, Statements, & Questions

After you have read this chapter, you should be able to define the terms/concepts, explain the statements, and answer the questions in this section *in your own words*. When appropriate, it may help to give a concrete example of the term or statement. It is most helpful if you try to answer in your own words before looking in the textbook.

1. science _____

_____

2. Psychology is the scientific study of behavior. _____

_____

3. Science can change fundamental ideas. _____

_____

4. Science produces change *and* progress. _____

_____

5. Science works because it is an efficient means for identifying and correcting false beliefs.

_____

_____

6. Science is not a set of laboratory procedures. _____

_____

7. Science constrains beliefs by evidence. _____

_____

8. Evidence that is incompatible with a scientific claim should challenge belief in that claim.

_____

_____

9. Science promotes human values. _____

_____

10. In a few sentences, what does it mean to say that "Science Works?" List the evidence that

supports this claim. _____

_____

_____

11. What are the two fundamental features or characteristics of science? How is science different

from other human activities, such as politics or art, in regard to these features? _____

_____

_____

12. What fundamental feature of science does the adoption of the heliocentric model of the solar

system illustrate? _____

_____

13. What fundamental feature of science does the Human Genome Project illustrate? _____

_____

14. List 10 commonly held beliefs about human behavior that the authors claim are wrong.

_____

_____

_____

_____

_____

15. What are the three basic standards for scientific belief? Give an example of a belief that meets these three standards. Give an example of one that doesn't. _____

_____

_____

_____

16. What evidence has led the authors to doubt the existence of "psychic phenomena?" How is this related to the basic standards for scientific belief? _____

_____

_____

17. What exactly does it mean to say that a hypothesis is falsifiable? Not falsifiable? _____

_____

_____

18. Why is falsifiability so important in science? _____

_____

19. What exactly does the term "objective" mean with regard to scientific observations? _____

_____

_____

_____

Expanding Your Knowledge and Understanding:
Sciences

1. How can both psychology and physics be sciences? Do they differ on any of the characteristics delineated in this chapter?

_____

_____

_____

_____

_____

_____

2. Evaluate astrology and graphology (the analysis of handwriting) in terms of the standards for scientific belief.

_____

_____

_____

_____

_____

_____

Testing Your Knowledge and Understanding: Multiple Choice Questions

1. How does science differ from other human endeavors?
   a. Science uses subjective measures of experimentation
   b. Scientific knowledge can change things for the better
   c. Unlike science, other endeavors are falsifiable
   d. Unlike science, other endeavors can change people's minds about salient things

2. Which student was wrong in the identification of standards for scientific beliefs?
   a. Joe: Scientific beliefs must have observable consequences that could show the belief to be wrong
   b. Steve: Scientific claims should be compatible with available empirical evidence
   c. Mike: As empirical evidence increases, one's acceptance of a belief should increase
   d. Chris: Only confirming evidence has a role in science

3. Prior to being accepted to law school, Perry had to take the LSAT because psychologists believe the performance on this exam _____ performance in law school.
   a. describes
   b. predicts
   c. improves
   d. controls

Applying Your Knowledge and Understanding: Challenge

When JoAnn's uncle, a geologist, learned that JoAnn was majoring in psychology, he called her and asked why she was not following in the family's footsteps and becoming a scientist. He commented that psychology was nothing more than everyday common sense. What should JoAnn say in defense of the assertion that "psychology *is* a science?"

_____

_____

_____

_____

_____

_____

ANSWERS

Multiple Choice

1. b
2. d
3. b

Chapter 2 -- A Powerful Way to Investigate Human Behavior Is by Making Measurements and Looking for Correlations among Them

(or How Psychologists Investigate Relationships)

Checking Your Knowledge: Terms, Statements, & Questions

After you have read this chapter, you should be able to define the terms/concepts, explain the statements, and answer the questions in this section *in your own words*. When appropriate, it may help to give a concrete example of the term or statement. It is most helpful if you try to answer in your own words before looking in the textbook.

1. correlation coefficient _____

_____

2. direction of relationship _____

_____

3. negative correlation _____

_____

4. phi _____

_____

5. positive correlation _____

_____

6. public verifiability _____

_____

7. relationship _____

_____

8. strength of relationship _____

_____

9. Observation and measurement are the basis for correlational research. _____

_____

_____

_____

10. Correlational research allows the determination of a relationship between attributes. _____

_____

_____

11. Ways to illustrate a correlation between attributes are (a) scatterplots _____

_____

   and (b) 2 x 2 tables _____

_____

12. Correlation coefficients are useful for making predictions about the two attributes considered.

_____

_____

13. What does it mean to say that "A powerful way to investigate human behavior is by making

   measurements and looking for correlations among them?" What exactly are "correlations"?

   Give a specific example of how correlations are used to study human behavior. _____

_____

_____

_____

14. Each single point in Figure 2.6 represents two scores for each boy. Three boys had TVVL

   scores of 8. What were their AGG scores? _____

15. Count the points in cell A of Figure 2.7 and verify that the count matches the frequency shown

   in Figure 2.3. _____

16. What does the text mean by 50/50 splits? _____

_____

17. Consider a 2 x 2 table with 50/50 splits. If the correlation between the two attributes involved is .90 and you use that correlation to make predictions, what percentage of the time would your predictions be correct?_____

18. How are correlation coefficients used in employment testing? _____

_____

Expanding Your Knowledge and Understanding: The Meaning of Correlation Coefficients

Explain using everyday words how to interpret the following hypothetical correlations. Be sure to address both the strength and the direction of the coefficients.

1. a correlation coefficient of +.82 between number of games a football team wins and the number of fans who attend the games

_____

_____

2. a correlation coefficient of -.02 between number of letters in one's first name and number of friends

_____

_____

3. a correlation coefficient of -.63 between size of long distance telephone bill and number of letters written to friends

_____

_____

4. a correlation coefficient of +.24 between annual income and amount of money spent on summer vacation

_____

_____

Testing Your Knowledge and Understanding:
Multiple Choice Questions

1. The most accurate prediction can be made using which of the following correlation coefficients?
   a. -1.69
   b. +2.24
   c. +.31
   d. -.66

2. The strength of a correlation coefficient is reflected in
   a. the number of attributes measured
   b. the sign of the coefficient
   c. the absolute value of the coefficient
   d. the inverse of the value of the coefficient

3. Correlation coefficients range from
   a. -1.00 to +1.00
   b. 0.00 to +1.00
   c. -10 to +10
   d. -2.00 to +2.00

4. Which of the following statements is most descriptive of a correlation of -.84 between mental ability and amount of caffeine consumed?
   a. as amount of caffeine intake increases, mental ability increases
   b. caffeine causes mental ability to decrease
   c. there is essentially no relationship between caffeine intake and mental ability
   d. as caffeine intake increases, mental ability decreases

5. Which statement reflects the most appropriate understanding of correlational research?
   a. Correlational research allows an individual to determine causation between attributes.
   b. A statistically significant correlation always has useful practical applications.
   c. A researcher who knows that two variables are correlated is able to make predictions about the occurrence of the two attributes.
   d. The direction of a correlation coefficient allows a researcher to see if two attributes are related.

Applying Your Knowledge and Understanding:
Conducting a Correlational Study

Children are increasingly testifying in court in criminal cases, civil cases, and child custody cases. Understanding leagalese -- the language used in the legal world and particularly courtrooms -- is difficult for children. Assume that you have been hired to conduct a study focusing on the relationship between age of child and knowledge of 20 legal terms used routinely in the courtroom.

You must determine how to measure the attributes in ways that are publicly verifiable and, after the data are collected, ascertain if there is a relationship between age of children and knowledge of legalese. As the researcher, you must complete the following steps.

1. How would you measure the children's age?

_____

_____

2. How would you measure understanding of legalese, such as "court," "prosecutor," "cross examination," and "jury?"

_____

_____

3. In addition to terms such as "court," "jury," and "judge," what other examples of legalese may young children encounter in the courtroom?

_____

_____

4. Below are hypothetical responses given by children of different ages. How would you score each response for understanding (i.e., gives an acceptable vs. not acceptable response) of legalese?

_____ court: where bad people are punished
_____ jury: a bracelet or necklace
_____ cross examination: give a mean test
_____ court: where I play basketball
_____ judge: the boss in the courtroom
_____ attorney: someone who helps you
_____ defendant: someone on trial
_____ jury: people who decide if you did wrong
_____ attorney: defends the accused
_____ alibi: a fib
_____ sentence: punishment in prison
_____ prosecutor: tries to put bad guy in prison
_____ swear: promises to do something
_____ alibi: telling where you were at the time of the crime
_____ sentence: a complete thought with a noun and a verb
_____ cross examination: the other side asks questions
_____ judge: to impose a value on others

Below is a hypothetical data set specifying the age of a child and the number of legal words or terms that child knew (i.e., judged to be an acceptable response).

Age (in years)	Number of words defined appropriately
3.0	3
3.5	2
3.5	4
3.5	3
4.0	3
4.0	4
4.5	4
5.0	5
5.0	3
5.5	7
5.5	8
5.5	6
6.0	8
6.0	7
6.5	9
6.5	7
7.0	6
7.0	10
7.5	6
7.5	8
7.5	9
8.0	5
8.0	6
8.5	10
9.0	14
9.0	15
9.5	12
9.5	13
10.0	16
10.0	14

5. Plot the data using a scatterplot.

6. Represent the data in a 2 x 2 table. How do you define the two levels of "age" and "number of words defined appropriately?" (In other words, how will you decide which quadrant of the 2 x 2 table each pair of data points goes into?)

7. Determine the correlation between age of children and number of legal words correctly understood.

   _____

8. Describe the relationship between age of child and understanding of legalese in everyday words.

   _____

   _____

9. What conclusions could you draw from this hypothetical study?

   _____

   _____

   _____

ANSWERS

The Meaning of Correlation Coefficients

1. As the number of football games won increases, the number of fans attending the games increases.
2. There is no relationship between number of letters in first name and number of friends.
3. As the size of the long distance bill increases, the number of letters written decreases.
4. As annual income increases, the amount of money spent on summer vacations increases.

Multiple Choice

1. d   2. c   3. a   4. d   5. c

Chapter 3 -- A Powerful Way to Investigate Human Behavior Is by Changing the Environment and Then Observing What Happens

(or How Psychologists Investigate Causal Relationships)

Checking Your Knowledge: Terms, Statements, & Questions

After you have read this chapter, you should be able to define the terms/concepts, explain the statements, and answer the questions in this section *in your own words*. When appropriate, it may help to give a concrete example of the term or statement. It is most helpful if you try to answer in your own words before looking in the textbook.

1. confounded _____

_____

2. control group _____

_____

3. dependent variable _____

_____

4. experiment _____

_____

5. experimental group _____

_____

6. independent variable _____

_____

7. random assignment _____

_____

8. random sampling _____

_____

9. Random assignment ensures that groups are comparable at the beginning of a study. _____

_____

_____

10. In an experimental study, only one aspect of the environment is manipulated at a time. _____

_____

_____

11. Confounding variables make it difficult to draw conclusions about the results. _____

_____

_____

12. Random sampling from a population allows generalization of findings back to that population.

_____

_____

13. Important effects generally have multiple causes. _____

_____

14. Important causes usually have multiple effects. _____

_____

15. Briefly summarize what it means to say that "One way to investigate human behavior is by

changing the environment and then observing what happens." Give a specific example of how

this approach is used to study human behavior. _____

_____

_____

_____

16. What does it mean to say that while causality implies correlation, correlation does not imply

causation? Why does correlational research usually not permit valid inferences to be made about causality? Why does experimental research often permit valid inferences about causality?

_____

_____

_____

_____

17. The word "experiment" is used in a variety of ways in everyday speech. What is its technical

meaning in this book? What are the main features of an experiment? What is the key difference

between experimental and correlational research? _____

_____

_____

_____

18. Why are research subjects assigned at random in experimental research? _____

_____

19. What is the difference between random sampling and random assignment? Which is critical in

allowing causal inferences? Which is critical in deciding on the generalizability of the results of

experiments? _____

_____

_____

20. List the five limitations of controlled experiments. _____

_____

_____

21. What did you learn in Part 1 (chapters 1, 2, and 3) that supports the Basic Idea that "science is

by far the most powerful way the human race has yet devised for understanding the world,

including, of course, our own behavior?" _____

_____

_____

_____

22. What did you learn in Part 1 that supports the Basic Idea that "humans have the ability to think

and reason in *very* powerful ways, but they also have a number of cognitive limitations that

lead to systematic errors?" _____

_____

_____

23. What did you learn in Part 1 that supports the Basic Idea that "many cognitive limitations can

be overcome by using cognitive tools?" _____

_____

_____

_____

Expanding Your Knowledge and Understanding: Independent and Dependent Variables

Identify what the independent variable (IV) and dependent variable (DV) would be if you were to design an experiment to test each of the following "hypotheses."

1. Boys don't make passes at girls who wear glasses.   IV: _____

    DV: _____

2. Too many cooks spoil the broth.   IV: _____

    DV: _____

3. Absence makes the heart grow fonder.   IV: _____

    DV: _____

4. You can't teach an old dog new tricks.   IV: _____

    DV: _____

5. An apple a day keeps the doctor away.   IV: _____

                                                  DV: _____

Expanding Your Knowledge and Understanding:
The Problem of Confounding

Professor Hack had always used a text called *The Best of Psychology* for his General Psychology classes. However, he saw a new text entitled *New Age Psychology* and wanted to compare student liking for the two textbooks. Since he taught two sections of General Psychology last semester, he decided to conduct an experiment to determine which was the better text. His first class, which met three times a week in the morning, had 30 female and 10 male students. For this class, he used his regular text, *The Best of Psychology*. His second class, which met Tuesday evening, had 5 female and 10 male students. For this class, Professor Hack used *New Age Psychology*. At the end of the semester, he had students in both classes rate their liking for the text they used. He found that *New Age Psychology* had a more positive rating, so he planning on using it exclusively in the future.

1. Did Professor Hack conduct an experiment? Explain your answer. _____

_____

_____

_____

2. What was the independent variable? _____

3. What was the dependent variable? _____

4. Was this a well-controlled study or did it suffer from confounding? If you think there was

   confounding, identify the confounding variable(s). _____

_____

_____

_____

5. Was Professor Hack justified in changing his textbook on the basis of these findings? Why or

   why not? _____

Testing Your Knowledge and Understanding:
Multiple Choice Questions

1. Ads for laundry detergents often claim that their detergents contain an ingredient that makes clothes whiter than the other brands lacking this secret ingredient. "Making clothes whiter" is
   a. the experimental condition
   b. the dependent variable
   c. the confounding variable
   d. the independent variable

2. Dependent variable is to independent variable as _____ is to _____
   a. measured; manipulated
   b. manipulated; measured
   c. control; experimental
   d. experimental; control

3. Who offered the best explanation of the primary advantage of experimental research?
   a. Jennifer: "It is the only way to determine if variables are related to each other."
   b. Kendra: "It is not restricted by the need to control variables."
   c. Jason: "It allows one to make causative statements."
   d. Sam: "It requires the elimination of independent variables."

4. A confounding variable is found in which if the following studies?
   a. a study comparing female part-time students with male full-time students
   b. a study comparing urban college students with rural college students
   c. a study comparing M.D.s with R.N.s
   d. a study comparing male bus drivers with male truck drivers

5. Students studying for a final exam got very confused and made the following statements. Who is likely to pass the exam?
   a. Billy: "Correlational research allows causal inferences to be made."
   b. Bob: "Random sampling has the same goal as random assignment."
   c. Carol: "Random assignment is crucial in the generalization of results to the population."
   d. Theresa: "The fact that one variable has a causal influence on another variable does not rule out other causal influences."

6. Which of the following students shows the best understanding of random assignment?
    a. Eddie: "Random assignment controls for unanticipated differences."
    b. Leo: "Random assignment controls for possible confounding variables that threaten an experiment."
    c. Ben: "Random assignment ensures that the experimental group is similar to the population to which the findings are to be generalized."
    d. Jordan: "Random assignment ensures that participants in two groups are identical on only critical characteristics."

7. If you are studying the effects of sleep deprivation on driving ability, the participants who are allowed to sleep are in the
    a. confounding group
    b. experimental group
    c. control group
    d. research group

8. Dr. Valdez believes that caffeine makes people aggressive. The best way to conduct an experiment focusing on this hypothesized relationship would be which of the following?
    a. Ask people how much caffeine they consume and then report how aggressive they have been over the last week.
    b. Assign people to one of four conditions of caffeine consumption and control caffeine intake appropriately while assessing their aggressiveness each day.
    c. Go to a coffee bar and see who drinks regular versus decaf coffee and interview the individuals in both groups about their aggressiveness.
    d. Have people complete a questionnaire about caffeine intake and then observe the people in a stressful situation.

Applying Your Knowledge and Understanding: Random Assignment

To see how random assignment makes two groups similar on both important and unimportant variables, try this exercise with the data set below. This data set includes two pieces of information for each participant: age (a variable frequently considered to be important in research) and number of letters in last name (a variable rarely considered to be important in research). This exercise will result in the completion of the table that follows the data set.

Data Set

Participant Number	Age	Letters in Last Name	Participant Number	Age	Letters in Last Name
1	27	6	26	44	8
2	35	6	27	36	9
3	29	4	28	23	8
4	41	7	29	41	19
5	46	6	30	22	8
6	19	8	31	49	8
7	42	5	32	27	5
8	43	6	33	42	4
9	35	4	34	28	6
10	29	5	35	33	9
11	30	7	36	31	15
12	25	5	37	37	11
13	21	6	38	22	6
14	40	5	39	29	5
15	33	9	40	26	10
16	23	6	41	33	4
17	36	5	42	47	7
18	44	9	43	20	7
19	39	9	44	29	8
20	20	8	45	34	4
21	22	11	46	21	8
22	36	10	47	49	11
23	31	5	48	39	6
24	42	10	49	42	4
25	37	7	50	40	10

Trial	Average Age		Average Letters	
	Group 1	Group 2	Group 1	Group 2
1				
2				
3				
4				

Trial 1: Assign all odd-numbered individuals to Group 1 and even-numbered individuals to Group 2. Then calculate the average age and average number of letters in last name for each group. Enter your results in the table above.

Trial 2: Assign the first half of the individuals to Group 1 and the second half to Group 2. Then calculate the average age and average number of letters in last name for each group. Enter your results in the table.

Trial 3: Random assignment of participants to the two groups will be completed by tossing a coin. Assign "heads" participants to Group 1 and "tails" participants to Group 2. Recalculate the average age and average number of letters in last name for each group. Then enter the results in the table.

Trial 4: Again, toss a coin to reassign the participants to the two groups. Recalculate the average age and average number of letters in last name for each group. Then enter the results in the table.

How comparable are the averages in each trial? Did random assignment essentially equate the two

groups? _____

_____

_____

_____

ANSWERS

Independent and Dependent Variables

1. IV: wearing glasses vs. not wearing glasses
2. IV: number of cooks
3. IV: absence vs. presence of person
4. IV: age of dog
5. IV: eating vs. not eating an apple

DV: number of passes
DV: quality of broth (taste)
DV: level of fondness
DV: performance of trick (learning)
DV: number of visits to the doctor

The Problem of Confounding

1. Although Professor Hack thought he was conducting an experiment, his study lacked random assignment. Thus, it was not an experiment.
2. IV: textbook used
3. DV: student liking
4. There is confounding. Possible confounding variables include scheduling of class (e.g., three times per week vs. once a week, morning vs. evening class), and student characteristics (e.g., gender of students, day vs. night students, total number of students in each class, ratio of men to women)
5. These findings do not justify changing the textbook.

Multiple Choice

1. b
2. a
3. c
4. a

5. d
6. a
7. c
8. b

Chapter 4 -- Much Human Behavior Is the Result of Both Long-Term and Short-Term Adaptations

(or Why Nature and Nurture Are Inextricably Intertwined)

Checking Your Knowledge:
Terms, Statements, & Questions

After you have read this chapter, you should be able to define the terms/concepts, explain the statements, and answer the questions in this section *in your own words*. When appropriate, it may help to give a concrete example of the term or statement. It is most helpful if you try to answer in your own words before looking in the textbook.

1. adaptation _____

   _____

2. fitness _____

   _____

3. natural selection _____

   _____

4. sociobiology _____

   _____

5. Long-term adaptations make short-term adaptations (both behavioral and physiological)

   possible. _____

   _____

6. Adaptations resulting in reproductive success increase the fitness of an organism. _____

   _____

   _____

7. The linking of evolution to human behavior (as in sociobiology and evolutionary psychology)

   has significant problems: (a) the genetic basis for any given human behavior cannot be

   demonstrated with a controlled experiment _____

and (b) because of the variability of human behavior, genetic influences on behavior may be less clear-cut and obvious than with other animals. _____

8. The evolutionary component to human behavior hinges on two factors: (a) the existence of cultural universals _____

and (b) the fitness of such cultural universals. _____

9. Learning is a short-term adaptation to a specific context. _____

10. What does it mean to say that "Much human behavior is the result of both long-term and short-term adaptations?" Give an example of a short-term adaptation. Give an example of a long-term adaptation. _____

11. Briefly summarize the kind of evidence that led Darwin to propose his theory of evolution.

12. What exactly does "fitness" mean in an evolutionary context? _____

13. Describe the role of individual differences in evolution. What does "fitness" mean in this context? _____

_____

_____

14. Behaviorism and sociobiology are radically different approaches to understanding human nature. What is the fundamental difference between them? _____

_____

_____

15. How does learning reflect both long-term and short-term adaptations? _____

_____

_____

16. Why do the authors avoid the term "instinct?" _____

_____

17. What does it mean to say that the expression of long-term adaptations is "context-specific?"

_____

_____

_____

Testing Your Knowledge and Understanding: Multiple Choice Questions

1. Which of the following is not a problem in the linking of evolution to human behavior?
   a. Human behavior is vastly more variable than the behavior of other animals.
   b. It cannot be demonstrated experimentally.
   c. Genetic predispositions lead to general behavior tendencies.
   d. Selective breeding of people is impossible.

2. Which student offered the best definition of evolutionary psychology?
   a. Matt: "It is the study of how instincts are manifested in people."
   b. Rudy: "It is the study of evolution in lower animals."
   c. Katie: "It is the study of environmental influences on behavior."
   d. Tony: "It is the application of sociobiology to the understanding of psychological phenomena."

Applying Your Knowledge and Understanding: Challenge

Sociobiology and evolutionary psychology have offered explanations for a variety of human behaviors. See how well you can do trying to explain how each of the following behaviors is the result of evolutionary adaptations.

1. Fear of snakes: _____

_____

_____

_____

2. Preference for food high in sugar and fat: _____

_____

_____

_____

3. Altruism: _____

_____

_____

_____

4. Need to affiliate with other people: _____

_____

_____

_____

ANSWERS

Multiple Choice

1. c
2. d

Chapter 5 -- Understanding the Brain Is the Foundation for Understanding the Mind

(or Why Biology and Psychology Are Inextricably Intertwined)

****Remember, the material in chapters 5 and 6 is more technical than the rest of the book, and is usually fairly difficult to understand for most people. What the authors suggest in the Introduction to Part 2 is definitely good advice -- you may need to read these chapters more than once before you have a grasp on them. This is also a good time to remind you that retention and understanding are much better if you can explain the material in your own words, so even though these terms and concepts may be difficult, try to get it on your own before simply copying definitions and answers from the textbook.****

Checking Your Knowledge:
Terms, Statements, & Questions

After you have read this chapter, you should be able to define the terms/concepts, explain the statements, and answer the questions in this section *in your own words*. When appropriate, it may help to give a concrete example of the term or statement. It is most helpful if you try to answer in your own words before looking in the textbook.

1. action potential

2. axon

3. brain stem

4. cerebral cortex

5. dendrites

6. excitation

7. inhibition _____

_____

8. limbic system _____

_____

9. neuron _____

_____

10. neurotransmitter _____

_____

11. old mammalian brain _____

_____

12. synapse _____

_____

13. synaptic gap _____

_____

14. Circuits consist of interconnected neurons and synaptic gaps and are very similar across many species. _____

_____

15. Communication is electrochemical within a neuron and chemical between neurons. _____

_____

_____

16. The action potential is the firing of a neuron. _____

_____

_____

17. Neurotransmitters include: (a) acetylcholine _____

(b) dopamine _____

(c) serotonin _____

(d) nitric oxide _____

(e) glutamate _____

18. What is the "neuron doctrine?" _____

_____

_____

_____

19. Describe how a nerve impulse progresses along a neuron. _____

_____

_____

_____

20. How are brains like computers? How are they unlike computers? _____

_____

_____

_____

21. What are the three components of the triune brain? _____

_____

22. What is the major functional difference between the right and left cerebral hemispheres?

_____

_____

_____

_____

23. What is meant by "open" and "closed" bioprograms? _____

_____

_____

_____

24. What is the fundamental difference between the kinds of research conducted by behaviorists

and by ethologists? _____

_____

_____

_____

Expanding Your Knowledge and Understanding:
Name the Location

Identify the location of the brain structures listed below and fill in the table on the next page.

amygdala   parietal lobe
cerebellum   pons
frontal lobe   reticular formation
hypothalamus   temporal lobe
medulla   thalamus
occipital lobe

Brain Stem	Limbic System	Cerebral Cortex
_____	_____	_____
_____	_____	_____
_____	_____	_____
_____		_____

Testing Your Knowledge and Understanding: Multiple Choice Questions

1. _____ store the neurotransmitters.
   a. Dendrites
   b. Axons
   c. Synapses
   d. Synaptic vesicles

2. The _____ is the space between neurons.
   a. axon
   b. dendrite
   c. synapse
   d. axial space

3. Which of the following is not a neurotransmitter?
   a. nitrous oxide
   b. glutamate
   c. acetylcholine
   d. dopamine

4. A loss of interest in food and possible starvation may result from damage to the
   a. amygdala
   b. medulla
   c. hypothalamus
   d. thalamus

5. Ray has damaged parietal lobes. As a result, he has trouble with
   a. vision
   b. touch
   c. hearing
   d. motor processes

6. _____ is to _____ as _____ is to _____.
   a. Temporal lobe; hearing; occipital lobe; vision
   b. Occipital lobe; hearing; frontal lobe; vision
   c. Frontal lobe; touch; parietal lobe; hearing
   d. Parietal lobe; motor processes; frontal lobe; touch

7. _____ receive messages from other neurons.
   a. Axons
   b. Neurotransmitters
   c. Dendrites
   d. Synapses

8. Which student has obviously not read this chapter yet?
   a. Martin: "Closed circuits allow little environmental modulation."
   b. Emily: "Open circuits are open to learning."
   c. Charlie: "Humans do not have instincts -- all behavior is learned."
   d. Will: "Much of the human cortex is multimodal."

9. If brain damage has left you feeling listless and without motivation, you have probably damaged your
   a. cerebellum
   b. temporal lobe
   c. limbic system
   d. thalamus

10. Steve and Laura were camping one night when Laura felt something crawling on her leg. She opened the sleeping bag, shined a light on her leg, and saw a scorpion. The sensation of the scorpion crawling on Laura's leg was registered on her _____ lobe.
    a. frontal
    b. temporal
    c. parietal
    d. occipital

11. If you damage your cerebellum, you are likely to have problems with
    a. long-term memory
    b. balance
    c. bodily sensations
    d. higher mental activity

Applying Your Knowledge and Understanding: Challenge

Attorneys for some individuals on trial for rape have argued that their clients should not be held legally responsible for their crimes because the behaviors were the product of structures in the old mammalian brain. According to these attorneys, the men's brains were essentially "pre-wired" for aggressive behavior and, thus, aggressive behavior was outside of the control of the men. If behavior is outside of the control of an individual, then that person is not legally responsible for the behavior.

1. How would an early ethologist respond to this argument? _____

_____

_____

_____

_____

2. How would a behaviorist respond to this argument? _____

_____

_____

_____

_____

3. How do *you* respond to this argument? _____

_____

_____

_____

_____

ANSWERS

Name the Location

Brain stem: medulla, pons, reticular formation, cerebellum

Limbic system: hypothalamus, thalamus, amygdala

Cerebral cortex: frontal lobe, occipital lobe, temporal lobe, parietal lobe

Multiple Choice

1. d	7. c
2. c	8. c
3. a	9. c
4. c	10. c
5. b	11. b
6. a	

Chapter 6 -- The Properties of the Mind Arise from Specific Circuits in the Brain

(or Why the Brain Is Not a Tabula Rasa)

Checking Your Knowledge:
Terms, Statements, & Questions

After you have read this chapter, you should be able to define the terms/concepts, explain the statements, and answer the questions in this section *in your own words*. When appropriate, it may help to give a concrete example of the term or statement. It is most helpful if you try to answer in your own words before looking in the textbook.

1. corpus callosum _____

_____

2. equipotential view _____

_____

3. lateralization of function _____

_____

4. localization view _____

_____

5. long-term adaptation _____

_____

6. short-term adaptation _____

_____

7. split brain _____

_____

8. Brain functions are localized. _____

9. In the memory process, (a) encoding of new experiences to long-term memory is done by the

hippocampus _____

_____

(b) storage occurs throughout the cerebral cortex _____

_____

and (c) retrieval is initiated, in part, by primitive sub-cortical pathways _____

_____

_____

10. Language is localized in the left cerebral hemisphere and involves: (a) Wernicke's Area _____

_____

_____

and (b) Broca's Area _____

_____

11. For most sensory information, input from the right side of the body goes to the left hemisphere and input from the left side of the body goes to the right hemisphere. _____

_____

_____

12. Split-brain research has shown that the left hemisphere is analytical and outward-directed and the right hemisphere is creative and inward-directed. _____

_____

_____

13. What does it mean to say that "some memory functions arise from specific circuits in the brain?" _____

_____

_____

14. Explain how language is processed in the brain. Is it localized completely in one hemisphere? Is it the same for both children and adults? _____

_____

_____

_____

15. What is the communication channel between the cerebral hemispheres that is severed in split-brain patients? Why is it easier to understand the effects of severing this channel when the patient's sense of smell is studied? _____

_____

_____

_____

16. Briefly summarize the differences found between the left and right hemispheres. _____

_____

_____

_____

_____

Expanding Your Knowledge and Understanding:
Figure It Out

Chad, an individual who has undergone a split-brain operation, agreed to participate in a demonstration. In the first phase of the demonstration, he was shown an umbrella. However, it was presented to him so that the visual input would go to only one hemisphere at a time.

1. If the input reached only the left hemisphere, would Chad be able to name the object? If so, why? If not, why not? _____

_____

_____

_____

_____

2. If the input reached only the right hemisphere, would Chad be able to name the object? If so,

why? If not, why not? _____

_____

_____

_____

3. If the input reached only the right hemisphere and he was presented with the following objects, identify two things Chad could do so that his left hemisphere knows he was presented with an umbrella:

book	picture of shoes
paper	picture of house
scissors	picture of can
pencil	picture of umbrella
clay	picture of cat

_____

_____

_____

_____

_____

Testing Your Knowledge and Understanding:
Multiple Choice Questions

1. For most people, language production is localized in the
   a. right hemisphere
   b. left hemisphere
   c. hippocampus
   d. corpus callosum

2. Severing the corpus callosum was a treatment for
   a. epilepsy
   b. schizophrenia
   c. depression
   d. anxiety disorders

3. Broca's Area is to Wernicke's Area as _____ is to _____.
   a. language production; language comprehension
   b. language comprehension; language production
   c. language formation; language production
   d. language production; language formation

4. If your right brain is damaged, the _____ part of your body would be most affected.
   a. right
   b. left
   c. upper
   d. lower

5. Which student has the best understanding of emotionality and brain hemispheres?
   a. Pat: "People with right hemisphere damage have catastrophic emotional responses."
   b. Phil: "People with left hemisphere damage have catastrophic emotional responses."
   c. Mary: "People with left hemisphere damage deny any major life changes."
   d. Lisa: "People with right hemisphere damage are very concerned about any major life changes."

6. After a stroke, Randy was unable to speak. However, his responses to even simple questions revealed that he did not understand the questions. His stroke most likely damaged his
   a. right hemisphere
   b. Wernicke's Area
   c. occipital lobe
   d. Broca's Area

7. With regard to data processing, the right hemisphere tends to be _____ and the left hemisphere tends to be _____.
   a. analytical; global
   b. global; analytical
   c. logical; global
   d. global; creative

8. After a car accident in which Gary suffered severe brain damage, he works the same jig-saw puzzle again and again -- never realizing that he just completed it before. He probably suffered damage to his
   a. corpus callosum
   b. hippocampus
   c. cingulate cortex
   d. arcuate fasciculus

9. _____ has been a means of studying lateralization.
   a. Arcuate fasciculus cuts
   b. Cingulate cortex surgery
   c. Split-brain surgery
   d. Equipotential surgery

Applying Your Knowledge and Understanding: Challenge

Guiseppe Arcimboldo (1527-1593), an Italian painter, produced remarkable portraits in which everyday objects were used in the creation of people. For example, in one portrait, stacks of books become a man. In others, vegetables, fruits, or flowers were positioned so they looked like people. Thus, the parts of the portrait can be perceived by themselves as objects completely independent of and unrelated to the portrait.

The portraits also allow a wonderful demonstration of the effects of split-brain on perception. Each portrait consists of two parts: the whole (i.e., the person) and its parts (i.e., the books, flowers, fruits, etc.). When the visual input from a portrait reaches both hemispheres, the individual is able to see both a person and the components used -- although not at the exact same time. However, given the lateralization of function in the brain, what would an individual perceive if the visual input was restricted to one hemisphere at a time? Would the person see the whole (the portrait), the parts (the books), or would she still be able to see both?

1. If the visual input from one of these portraits is presented to the left hemisphere only, what

   would that person say she saw? Why? _____

_____

_____

_____

_____

2. If the visual input from one of these portraits is presented to the right hemisphere only, what

would that person say she saw? Why? _____

_____

_____

_____

_____

_____

_____

ANSWERS

Figure It Out

1. If the input reached only the left hemisphere, Chad would be able to say "umbrella" since the left hemisphere is where speech is located for most people.

2. For the same reason, if the input reached only the right hemisphere, Chad would be unable to say "umbrella."

3. If provided with the material on the list and the input reached only the right hemisphere, Chad could point to the picture of the umbrella or, with paper and pencil, he could draw an umbrella with his left hand (even if he is right-handed).

Multiple Choice

1. b   6. b
2. a   7. b
3. a   8. b
4. b   9. c
5. b

Challenge

1. If the visual input from one of these portraits reached only the left hemisphere, the individual would report seeing books, fruits, or flowers -- whichever was used in that portrait. The left hemisphere is analytical.

2. If the visual input from one of these portraits reached only the right hemisphere, the individual would report seeing a portrait. The right hemisphere is global. In fact, facial recognition is a right brain function.

Chapter 7 -- Some Male--Female Differences Are the Result of Long-Term Adaptations

(or Why Nearly All the Clients of Prostitutes Are Male)

Checking Your Knowledge:
Terms, Statements, & Questions

After you have read this chapter, you should be able to define the terms/concepts, explain the statements, and answer the questions in this section *in your own words*. When appropriate, it may help to give a concrete example of the term or statement. It is most helpful if you try to answer in your own words before looking in the textbook.

1. polyandry _____

_____

2. polygyny _____

_____

3. sociobiology _____

_____

4. Different male--female mating strategies are apparent in human sexual behavior. _____

_____

_____

5. Reasons underlying these mating differences include: (a) the relative biological contributions of

women and men _____

_____

(b) copulation has greater consequences for women than for men _____

_____

and (c) a woman is biologically guaranteed that her children carry her genes _____

_____

6. The differential mating strategies are based on maximizing fitness and passing genes on to

subsequent generations: (a) for males, the strategy is to copulate as often and as indiscriminately as possible _____

_____

_____

and (b) for females, the strategy is to copulate occasionally and selectively _____

_____

_____

7. There are other gender differences in mating strategies that are consistent with natural selection:

(a) polygyny is more common than polyandry _____

_____

_____

(b) men engage in sexual activity more frequently than do females _____

_____

_____

(c) males pay for sex but females rarely do _____

_____

_____

(d) men use physical force to have sex but females rarely do _____

_____

_____

(e) females are more discriminating than men in sexual partner selection _____

_____

_____

8. What does it mean to say that "Some male--female differences are the result of long-term adaptations?" Briefly summarize the evidence that supports this claim. _____

_____

_____

_____

9. In Chapter 4, it was argued that there were two basic issues that need to be examined when some particular human behavior is claimed to have an evolutionary basis. What were these two issues? How does the claim that some male--female differences are the result of long-term adaptations fare in regard to these two issues? _____

_____

_____

_____

_____

10. Is the evidence for gender differences in reaction to emotional vs. sexual affairs by a partner based on experimental or correlational research? Would it be possible to study this question with either type of research? Why or why not? _____

_____

_____

_____

11. How does the concept of fitness apply to Tinbergen's research with stickleback fish? _____

_____

_____

12. According to sociobiology, why is there a tendency for women to be more discriminating than men about whom they have sex with? _____

_____

_____

_____

_____

13. According to sociobiology, why is there a tendency for men to be more upset than women by

their partners' having a sexual affair? _____

_____

_____

14. What are the major objections to sociobiological explanations of male--female differences in

sexual behavior? What counter-arguments does the text propose to these objections? _____

_____

_____

_____

_____

15. What did you learn in Part 2 (chapters 4, 5, 6, and 7) to support the Basic Idea that "adaptation

is *the* fundamental property of human behavior and cognition?" _____

_____

_____

_____

_____

16. What did you learn in Part 2 to support the Basic Idea that "one cannot understand psychology

without understanding evolution. *Much* human behavior results from an interaction between

genetic factors and the immediate situation?" _____

_____

_____

_____

Expanding Your Knowledge and Understanding:
Sexual Aggression

Some evolutionary psychologists have suggested that rape is the result of evolution -- men use physical force as a way to achieve intercourse and, consequently, the opportunity to procreate.

1. Do you think rape is the result of sexual desires, aggressive desires, or a combination of the

   two? _____

   _____

   _____

2. If a man rapes as a result of the predisposition in men to pass on their genes, should he be held

   legally responsible for this behavior? _____

   _____

   _____

Testing Your Knowledge and Understanding:
Multiple Choice Questions

1. Which of the following is <u>not</u> one of the reasons identified in the text as explaining underlying gender differences in mating behaviors?
   a. sperm are cheap and eggs are expensive
   b. women have a nine-month biological "time-out" from procreation while pregnant
   c. women have a guarantee that their children carry their genes
   d. across all cultures for which we have data, women are more likely than men to have multiple spouses

2. Which student failed to offer a valid gender difference in mating strategies?
   a. Wendy: "Men are more sexually active than women."
   b. Brendon: "Polyandry is more common than polygyny."
   c. Michael: "Most prostitutes in the United States are women with men as clients."
   d. Marty: "Almost all rapists are males."

Applying Your Knowledge and Understanding: Challenge

There are other gender differences for which sociobiology and evolutionary psychology have offered explanations. See how well you can do trying to explain how each of the following behaviors is the result of evolutionary adaptations.

1. Greater aggressiveness in males _____

_____

_____

_____

_____

2. Men's greater strength in map reading _____

_____

_____

_____

_____

3. Women's better memory for locales _____

_____

_____

_____

_____

4. Men's greater maze learning _____

_____

_____

_____

_____

ANSWERS

Multiple Choice

1. d
2. b

Chapter 8 -- We Respond to Change, but We Adapt to Lack of Change

(or Why You Notice Your Refrigerator Only When It Starts or Stops Running)

Checking Your Knowledge:
Terms, Statements, & Questions

After you have read this chapter, you should be able to define the terms/concepts, explain the statements, and answer the questions in this section *in your own words*. When appropriate, it may help to give a concrete example of the term or statement. It is most helpful if you try to answer in your own words before looking in the textbook.

1. adaptation

2. cones

3. hedonic adaptation

4. just noticeable difference (jnd)

5. kinesthesis

6. rods

7. tympanic membrane

8. Weber's Law

9. Adaptation is a change in sensitivity to stimulation or an overt responding to changing environmental situations.

_____

_____

10. Adaptation has survival value. _____

_____

11. Adaptation keeps us responsive to novelty. _____

_____

12. Adaptation can lead to a sense of relative deprivation. _____

_____

13. Our various senses respond to change. _____

_____

14. Chemical changes caused by changes in electromagnetic radiation stimulate visual receptors.

_____

15. Rods and cones have specialized roles in vision. _____

_____

16. Retinal images do not match the external environment. _____

_____

17. Changes in pressure of air molecules are the environmental triggers for hearing. _____

_____

_____

18. Sound waves cause the tympanic membrane to vibrate and those vibrations are converted into

neural impulses. _____

_____

_____

19. Hair cells are the actual hearing receptors. _____

_____

_____

20. Changes in pressure are the environmental events that trigger touch. _____

_____

_____

21. A good analogy for the nervous system may be the digital computer. _____

_____

_____

22. Describe, in one sentence each, two sensory systems other than vision, audition, taste, smell,

and touch. _____

_____

_____

23. How would you test Weber's Law for the loudness of sound? _____

_____

_____

24. What are the receptors for vision? Audition? (No, not the eyes and ears...) _____

_____

_____

_____

_____

25. What is a "distance sense?" _____

_____

_____

26. What does the expression "We live in a sea of energy" mean? What other products of

technology show that "we live in a sea of energy?" _____

_____

_____

_____

27. Describe the flow of information from a visual to the brain. _____

_____

_____

28. What is a "mechanoreceptor?" _____

_____

_____

29. What are the three different usages of the term "adaptation?" _____

_____

_____

_____

30. What is the anatomical reason for the blind spot? _____

_____

_____

31. List some costs and benefits of sensory adaptation. _____

_____

_____

_____

32. Explain how complex systems can arise from simple elements. _____

_____

_____

_____

Expanding Your Knowledge and Understanding: A Perception Puzzle

Read the clues below and write the responses in the spaces provided. Then insert the letters from the numbered spaces into the appropriate spaces in the puzzle. The answer is a statement about sensation and perception.

$\overline{1}\ \overline{2}\ \overline{3}\qquad \overline{4}\ \overline{5}\ \overline{6}\ \overline{7}\ \overline{8}\ \overline{9}\qquad \overline{10}\ \overline{11}\ \overline{12}\ \overline{13}\ \overline{14}\ \overline{15}\ \overline{16}$

$\overline{17}\ \overline{18}\ \overline{19}\ \overline{20}\ \overline{21}\ \overline{22}\ \overline{23}\ \overline{24}\ \overline{25}\qquad \overline{26}\ \overline{27}\qquad \overline{28}\ \overline{29}\ \overline{30}\ \overline{31}\ \overline{32}\ \overline{33}$

1. a blind spot in the visual field

$\overline{27}\ \overline{\ }\ \overline{\ }\ \overline{\ }\qquad \overline{6}\ \overline{\ }\ \overline{\ }\ \overline{\ }\ \overline{33}$

2. allows you to tell if something is red or blue

$\overline{28}\ \overline{\ }\ \overline{\ }\ \overline{5}\ \overline{\ }$

3. responsible for vision that helps you avoid traffic when crossing the street

$\overline{22}\ \overline{\ }\ \overline{\ }\ \overline{4}$

4. condition in which a person cannot name an object by touching it and manipulating it in his or her hand

$\overline{\ }\ \overline{32}\ \overline{\ }\ \overline{\ }\ \overline{\ }\ \overline{\ }\ \overline{\ }$

5. the highs and lows of sound

$\overline{13}\ \overline{\ }\ \overline{26}\ \overline{\ }\ \overline{\ }$

55

6. home of auditory receptors
— — $\overline{9}$ — — $\overline{21}$ —

— — — — $\overline{18}$ — $\overline{15}$ —

7. tympanic membrane
— — — $\overline{16}$ — — $\overline{20}$

8. _____ on the skin begins a squeeze
$\overline{17}$ $\overline{10}$ — — — $\overline{2}$ — $\overline{8}$

9. this lets you know the position of
your arms in space even when you
cannot see them
— $\overline{23}$ — $\overline{11}$ — — $\overline{29}$ — — — —

10. damage to these causes balance
problems
$\overline{7}$ — — $\overline{19}$ — — — — — $\overline{24}$ — $\overline{3}$

— — — — — $\overline{12}$

11. this says the just noticeable difference
is a constant percentage of the original
stimulus
— — — — — ' — — $\overline{30}$ —

12. visual center in the brain
$\overline{14}$ — — — — — — — —

— $\overline{1}$ — — — —

13. area of the brain that
processes touch
— — — — — — — — $\overline{31}$ — — — $\overline{25}$

Testing Your Knowledge and Understanding:
Multiple Choice Questions

1. Sensory adaptation refers to a(n)
   a. increase in sensitivity
   b. decline in sensitivity
   c. broadening of perceptual experiences
   d. sensory overload

2. Which of the following is not an example of sensory adaptation?
   a. getting used to the sound of dripping water
   b. getting accustomed to your cat sitting on your lap
   c. hearing your name spoken in a noisy room
   d. not noticing a well-used litter box

3. In his lecture on the process of adaptation in vision, Dr. Simpson explained that dark adaptation, a process that requires about 30 minutes to complete, allows you to see in a dark room. In this process, there is an imbalance between the breakdown and restoration of photochemicals -- they are being broken down but not restored. In contrast to dark adaptation, the complimentary process of light adaptation takes less time to occur. What statement should he have made instead of one he did make?
   a. The completion of dark adaptation requires only 15 to 20 minutes.
   b. Light adaptation actually requires more time than dark adaptation.
   c. Photochemicals are actually being restored but not broken down.
   d. Light adaptation is not a complementary process to dark adaptation.

4. Last year, Sarah and Tom built their dream house. It was a bit smaller than they had wanted, but the best they could afford. They have told all their friends that it is the perfect house -- that there couldn't be a better house for them. Last week, Sarah and Tom visited friends who just moved in to a much larger house with a swimming pool. If adaptation to their house has occurred, how are Sarah and Tom most likely to respond?
   a. They will think their house is still the perfect house.
   b. They will think their friends were garish for buying a house that was larger than they needed.
   c. They will discuss the dangers of having a swimming pool.
   d. They will see their house as insufficiently small for their own needs.

5. When Neil picks up his girlfriend, he overwhelms her with his cologne -- the aftershave that she likes best. However, he fails to understand why she complains about his cologne, particularly since she bought it for him. What is the problem?
   a. Neil has experienced adaptation to the smell but his girlfriend has not.
   b. Neil has experienced increased sensitivity but his girlfriend has experienced adaptation to the smell.
   c. Neil has experienced accommodation to the smell but his girlfriend has experienced homeostasis.
   d. Neil has experienced homeostasis but his girlfriend has experienced accommodation to the smell.

6. Which of the following combinations is correct?
   a. cones -- night vision
   b. rods -- daylight color vision
   c. pitch -- variation in sound frequency
   d. loudness -- complexity

7. _____ is determined by _____ and _____ is determined by _____.
   a. pitch, frequency; loudness, amplitude
   b. loudness, frequency; pitch, amplitude
   c. timbre, amplitude; pitch, frequency
   d. loudness, amplitude; timbre, frequency

8. Which of the following statements is true about vision?
   a. A blind spot in the visual field is in the lower part of the retina.
   b. Vision is the only sense that does not have a crossing pattern between side of information intake and the brain.
   c. How we see colors is completely understood.
   d. We move our eyes automatically and continuously.

9. Which of the following is not located in the middle ear?
   a. anvil
   b. stirrup
   c. cochlea
   d. hammer

10. Found in the _____, the _____ are responsible for _____.
   a. retina; cones; visual acuity
   b. retina; rods; color vision
   c. cochlea; hair cells; kinesthesia
   d. inner ear; Pacinian corpuscles; kinesthesia

11. A person who has difficulty seeing in dimly lit areas may have
   a. cones that are malfunctioning
   b. a particularly large blind spot
   c. rods that are malfunctioning
   d. a slow processing of visual information

12. When a police officer makes a suspected drunk driver attempt to touch his or her nose with both index fingers while the eyes are closed, the officer is testing which sense?
   a. touch
   b. vestibular
   c. perceptual
   d. kinesthetic

13. Even though a guitar, a flute, and a piano play the same notes at the same loudness, they sound differently as a result of a difference in
   a. timbre
   b. pitch
   c. tone
   d. frequency

Applying Your Knowledge and Understanding: Challenge

1. Information from the left visual field goes to the right brain and from the right visual field to the left brain. What hearing difficulty would you have if information from the left ear went only to the right brain and from the right ear only to the left brain? _____

_____

_____

_____

_____

2. Suppose you have a really nice dorm room or apartment, and you're quite happy with it. What happens when you visit a friend and he or she has a much nicer room or apartment? _____

_____

_____

_____

_____

ANSWERS

A Perception Puzzle

1. optic nerve
2. cones
3. rods
4. agnosia
5. pitch
6. basilar membrane
7. eardrum
8. pressure
9. kinesthesis
10. semicircular canals
11. Weber's Law
12. occipital cortex
13. somatosensory

Multiple Choice

1. b
2. c
3. c
4. d
5. a
6. c
7. a
8. d
9. c
10. a
11. c
12. d
13. a

Chapter 9 -- How We See the World Is Determined Both by What's Outside in the Environment and by What's Inside Us

(or Why Reality, Like Beauty, Is Partly in the Eye of the Beholder)

Checking Your Knowledge: Terms, Statements, & Questions

After you have read this chapter, you should be able to define the terms/concepts, explain the statements, and answer the questions in this section *in your own words*. When appropriate, it may help to give a concrete example of the term or statement. It is most helpful if you try to answer in your own words before looking in the textbook.

1. bottom-up processing _____

_____

2. closure _____

_____

3. Ebbinghaus illusion _____

_____

4. Gestalt psychologists _____

_____

5. good continuation _____

_____

6. Kanisza figure _____

_____

7. Müller-Lyer illusion _____

_____

8. Necker cube _____

_____

9. Ponzo illusion   _____

_____

10. proximity   _____

_____

11. reversible figure   _____

_____

12. similarity   _____

_____

13. top-down processing   _____

_____

14. Zollner illusion   _____

_____

15. A fundamental principle of perception is that, at any given time, our perception of a stimulus is restricted to one interpretation. _____

_____

16. Perceptions are influenced by the temporal contexts, including immediate and long-term past experiences. _____

_____

17. Perceptual pathologies are evidence that central psychological processes influence our perceptions. _____

_____

18. Simplification and representation are essential in the process of perception. _____

_____

_____

19. What is the distinction between "top-down" and "bottom-up" processes? _____

_____

20. What is the difference between an illusion and a hallucination? _____

_____

21. Which illusions in the chapter violate the laws of perspective? _____

_____

22. Which illusions are explained by the laws of perspective? _____

_____

23. This chapter showed a lot of examples in which our senses were fooled. Can we usually trust our senses to give us a useful representation of the world? _____

_____

24. If you are looking at a person's face, the face is in sharp focus. Everything else is out of focus. That is an example of what principle of perception? _____

_____

25. What is the difference between spatial context and temporal context? _____

_____

Expanding Your Knowledge and Understanding: Application to Other Senses

An understanding of the various processes and principles introduced in this chapter should enable you to apply them to senses other than vision. See if you can fill in the table below by writing examples in each box.

Sense

Process or Principle	Audition	Olfactory	Taste	Touch
Top-Down Processing				
Bottom-Up Processing				
Figure-Ground				
Proximity				
Similarity				
Closure				
Good Continuation				

Testing Your Knowledge and Understanding:
Multiple Choice Questions

1. Which of the following students did not read this chapter very well?
   a. Chris: "In top-down processing, an observer begins looking at the top of an object and works down, integrating new features of the object as they are encountered."
   b. Allie: "Perceptions are determined by both the object and our psychological processes."
   c. Daniel: "Illusions are good examples of how spatial contexts influence perception."
   d. Greg: "Even with reversible figures, you can see them in only one way in any given moment."

2. Three of the following assist in the perception of the fourth. Which is the fourth?
   a. similarity
   b. percept
   c. closure
   d. proximity

3. David sees the following as columns of S's, T's,   S   T   A   N
   A's, and N's rather than rows of the name "Stan."   S   T   A   N
   What Gestalt principle explains his perception?   S   T   A   N
   a. figure-ground
   b. closure
   c. similarity
   d. good continuation

4. Which of the following does not belong with the other three?
   a. closure
   b. good continuation
   c. disparity
   d. proximity

5. Whether "O" is perceived as a letter or a number in the following example depends upon what?
         M   N   O   P   Q
        -2   -1   O   +1   +2
   a. good continuation
   b. spatial context
   c. reversibility
   d. figure-ground

6. The importance of temporal context in perception
   a. is limited to immediate experiences
   b. is limited to recent past experiences
   c. includes only immediate recent past experiences
   d. includes but is not limited to long-term past experiences

7. Which of these is most closely associated with Gestalt psychology?
   a. extinction
   b. "the whole is greater than the sum of the parts"
   c. Müller-Lyer illusion
   d. size-distance theory

8. When adults holding a baby are told that the baby is a boy, they see the baby as more active, stronger, and louder. However, when the same baby is identified as a girl, adults perceive the baby as softer, more delicate, and more still. These two different perceptions of the same baby demonstrate the influence of _____ on perception.
   a. context
   b. similarity
   c. bottom-up processing
   d. emotion

Applying Your Knowledge and Understanding: Challenge

Some clinical psychologists use Rorschach cards or inkblots in their assessment of clients. Clients are asked to tell what they "see" in each inkblot. This task is very similar to lying on the lawn and "seeing" things in the clouds. Explain the role of each of the following in "seeing" things in an inkblot.

1. Top-down processing: _____

_____

_____

_____

2. Bottom-up processing: _____

_____

_____

_____

3. Figure-ground: _____

_____

_____

_____

4. Proximity: _____

_____

_____

_____

5. Similarity: _____

_____

_____

_____

6. Closure: _____

_____

_____

_____

7. Good continuation: _____

_____

_____

_____

ANSWERS

Multiple Choice

1. a	3. c	5. b	7. b
2. b	4. c	6. d	8. a

Chapter 10 -- We *Learn* to Perceive the World

(or Why a New Style of Music Sounds Strange--at First)

Checking Your Knowledge:
Terms, Statements, & Questions

After you have read this chapter, you should be able to define the terms/concepts, explain the statements, and answer the questions in this section *in your own words*. When appropriate, it may help to give a concrete example of the term or statement. It is most helpful if you try to answer in your own words before looking in the textbook.

1. congenital achromatopsia   _____

_____

2. perceptual learning   _____

_____

3. Speech perception is a powerful illustration of perceptual learning. _____

_____

_____

4. Why was Oliver Sacks so interested in going to the island of Pingelap? _____

_____

_____

5. When they arrived on Pingelap, Nordby noticed something about the children that Sacks and

Wasserman didn't. What was it? _____

_____

6. Why did Nordby notice it and Sacks and Wasserman didn't? _____

_____

_____

_____

7. About a year or so after Mr. I, the artist, became color blind, he began to adapt to his world without colors. How did he adapt? _____

_____

_____

_____

8. What happened when George Stratton first put on his image-inverting lenses? Describe his experiences. _____

_____

_____

_____

9. After wearing the lenses for a while, what happened to Stratton's visual perception? Describe his experiences then. _____

_____

_____

_____

10. What happened after he took the lenses off at the end of the second, 8-day experiment? _____

_____

_____

_____

Expanding Your Knowledge and Understanding: Learning to Speak E-Mail

With the steady increase in the use of the internet, and in particular, e-mail and "instant messaging," there has been a new "shorthand" system for certain expressions. For example, in my own experience, LOL means "laugh out loud," BTW means "by the way," and IMHO means "in my humble opinion." (BTW, do you use the same symbols in your e-mail? What other phrases are shortened in your e-mail "perceptual system?") Not to mention the existence of an entire new language of "smiley faces" meant to convey just about every emotion (or "emoticon") one could possibly have.

1. How do you think a new e-mail user interprets these symbols? Have you ever tried to teach someone how to use a new e-mail system?

_____

_____

_____

_____

2. How would someone who has been using e-mail and instant messaging for a few years interpret these symbols?

_____

_____

_____

_____

3. Is this a kind of perceptual learning? If so, why?

_____

_____

_____

_____

_____

Testing Your Knowledge and Understanding:
Multiple Choice Questions

1. Which is the best definition of perceptual learning?
   a. an increase in the ability to perceive objects in one's immediate environment
   b. an increase in the ability to extract information from the environment, as a result of experience and practice with stimulation coming from it
   c. adopting new skills as a result of reinforcement and punishment that come from the environment
   d. adapting to new ways of perceiving the environment as a result of classically conditioned responses to the environment

2. How did James, the guide from Pingelap, demonstrate that he (along with other islanders with achromatopsia) learned to perceive ripe bananas differently than color "normals" did?
   a. He knew they were ripe by the differences in shades of gray he saw in them.
   b. He always knew which people with normal color vision would tell him which bananas were ripe.
   c. He didn't know which were ripe, so he was never able to eat bananas.
   d. He knew they were ripe by looking at them, feeling them, and smelling them.

Applying Your Knowledge and Understanding:
A Perceptual Learning Exercise

Turn your computer mouse upside down so that if the mouse is moved to the right, the cursor moves to the left, and a move of the mouse away from you moves the cursor downward.

1. How well can you use the mouse initially? What sorts of problems do you have? _____

_____

_____

_____

2. How long does it take you to learn to use the upside-down mouse? _____

_____

3. When you turn the mouse right side up again, how long does it take you to readjust to using it? Do you have any problems readjusting?

_____

_____

_____

_____

ANSWERS

Multiple Choice

1. b
2. d

Chapter 11 -- There Is No Credible Evidence for *Extra*sensory Perception

(or Why Nobody Has Collected the Amazing Randi's Million Dollars)

Checking Your Knowledge:
Terms, Statements, & Questions

After you have read this chapter, you should be able to define the terms/concepts, explain the statements, and answer the questions in this section *in your own words*. When appropriate, it may help to give a concrete example of the term or statement. It is most helpful if you try to answer in your own words before looking in the textbook.

1. clairvoyance _____

_____

2. extrasensory perception _____

_____

3. paranormal phenomena _____

_____

4. psychokinesis _____

_____

5. telepathy _____

_____

6. Research offers no support for parapsychological claims. _____

_____

7. Reasons people believe in paranormal phenomena include: (a) expectations affect what people

see _____

_____

    (b) coincidences happen more often than people think they do _____

_____

and (c) people attach too much importance to single events _____

_____

8. When examining a possible relationship between two variables (as in the example given in the text of the "premonitions" of the teenagers' parents and whether an accident had occurred), why is any *single* positive hit meaningless in the absence of information about all four categories of the 2 x 2 table? (It may be helpful to work through that example in the text again to understand the general conclusion here.)

_____

_____

_____

_____

9. What did you learn in Part 3 (chapters 8, 9, 10, and 11) that supports the Basic Idea that

"perception is active, not passive. We *construct* internal representations of the external world,

but we don't just make them up?" _____

_____

_____

_____

10. What did you learn in Part 3 that supports the Basic Idea that "adaptation is *the* fundamental

property of human behavior and cognition?" _____

_____

_____

_____

11. What did you learn in Part 3 that supports the Basic Idea that "you cannot understand

psychology without understanding evolution. *Much* human behavior results from an interaction

between genetic factors and the immediate situation?" _____

_____

_____

_____

_____

12. What did you learn in Part 3 that supports the Basic Idea that "much human behavior results

from an interaction between past experience and the immediate situation?" _____

_____

_____

_____

13. What did you learn in Part 3 that supports the Basic Idea that "humans have the ability to think

and reason in *very* powerful ways, but we also have a number of cognitive limitations that lead

to systematic errors?" _____

_____

_____

_____

_____

Expanding Your Knowledge and Understanding: Belief in Precognition

This morning, your neighbor Betty came to your house and told you how awful she feels. A friend of hers was in a horrible accident and was in the hospital. Betty feels as if she is to blame because two days previously, she had had a dream about just such an accident. Betty tells you she feels so guilty because she had not called and warned her friend. She was certain if she had just called, then her friend would have stayed home and would not have been in the accident.

Another neighbor, Sally, said that she understood exactly how Betty felt. Sally explained that she had a similar dream about her daughter and made her stay home one night instead of going on a planned date. That very night her daughter's boyfriend was seriously injured in an accident.

How do you explain your two neighbors' experiences? What suggestions would you give them?

_____

_____

_____

_____

_____

Testing Your Knowledge and Understanding:
Multiple Choice Questions

1. Initial research on psi phenomena was mixed, but more recent improved research techniques have resulted in
   a. even more support for parapsychology
   b. replication of earlier findings
   c. less support for parapsychology
   d. more confusion about psi phenomena

2. _____ is the ability to perceive an event at a distance.
   a. Precognition
   b. Telepathy
   c. Psychokinesis
   d. Clairvoyance

3. All but _____ are examples of paranormal phenomena.
   a. precognition
   b. meditation
   c. telepathy
   d. psychokinesis

4. Many paranormal phenomena are the result of
   a. hard practice
   b. honed skills
   c. coincidence
   d. subliminal processes

5. Your friend tells you that her ESP allows her to know exactly what you are thinking. She is claiming she has
   a. clairvoyance
   b. telepathy
   c. precognition
   d. psychokinesis

6. Which student failed to offer a reason why most psychologists are skeptical about parapsychology?
   a. Karen: "There has not yet been any scientific replication of such phenomena."
   b. Jill: "The demonstrations of such phenomena are outside a controlled setting."
   c. Joe: "Most people refuse to admit that they have ESP."
   d. Brian: "Oftentimes claims of ESP have been found to be fraudulent."

7. What is one reason many people believe in paranormal phenomena?
   a. What they see challenges what they believe.
   b. Scientific data have supported that belief.
   c. They believe they have ESP.
   d. They attach too much importance to a single event.

Applying Your Knowledge and Understanding: Challenges

1. There is currently a large market for so-called "psychics" and "spiritual mediums" who claim they can see and receive messages from deceased loved ones. If you've ever seen one of these people on TV or in person, what kinds of things do they do to convince people of their "powers," but that any good magician could also do? If you were there in person, what might you, as a skeptic, do to try to "debunk" the "psychic?"

_____

_____

_____

_____

_____

2. Design an experiment that would allow you to test someone's claim that he receives mental messages from other people.

Experimental condition: _____

_____

Control condition: _____

_____

Independent variable: _____

_____

Dependent variable: _____

_____

Procedure: _____

_____

_____

_____

Expected findings: _____

_____

ANSWERS

Multiple Choice

1. c   5. b
2. d   6. c
3. b   7. d
4. c

Chapter 12 -- The Brain Is Programmed to Form Associations

(or Why People Salivate at the Smell of Burning Charcoal)

Checking Your Knowledge:
Terms, Statements, & Questions

After you have read this chapter, you should be able to define the terms/concepts, explain the statements, and answer the questions in this section *in your own words*. When appropriate, it may help to give a concrete example of the term or statement. It is most helpful if you try to answer in your own words before looking in the textbook.

1. acquisition curve

2. classical conditioning

3. conditioned response

4. conditioned stimulus

5. discrimination

6. extinction

7. generalization

8. neutral stimulus

9. spontaneous recovery

10. unconditioned response _____

_____

11. unconditioned stimulus _____

_____

12. Learning is a relatively permanent change in behavior based on experience. _____

_____

_____

13. An essential feature of learning is the forming of associations. _____

_____

_____

14. In classical conditioning, learning is best if the unconditioned stimulus comes after the neutral stimulus and if the interval between the two is brief. _____

_____

_____

15. Usually multiple pairings of the neutral and unconditioned stimuli are needed for learning to occur. _____

_____

_____

16. After a conditioned response has been learned, it can disappear as a result of extinction and reappear through spontaneous recovery. _____

_____

_____

17. Fear and anxiety responses are commonly learned via classical conditioning. _____

_____

18. For the conditioned eyeblink example, specify the following: the neutral stimulus, the unconditioned stimulus, the conditioned stimulus, the unconditioned response, and the conditioned response. _____

_____

_____

19. Why did Pavlov have the dog in a restraining harness? _____

_____

_____

20. How would you demonstrate generalization using the conditioned eyeblink response? _____

_____

_____

21. How would you demonstrate discrimination using the conditioned eyeblink response? _____

_____

_____

22. How would you demonstrate spontaneous recovery using the conditioned eyeblink response?

_____

_____

23. What is the difference between Rescorla and Wagner's (1972) research on predictability and Pavlov's on experimental neuroses? They both used random pairings of the conditioned and unconditioned stimuli. _____

_____

_____

_____

Expanding Your Knowledge and Understanding:
Name That Element

For each of the following classically conditioned behaviors, identify the unconditioned stimulus (UCS), conditioned stimulus (CS), unconditioned response (UCR), and conditioned response (CR).

1. Every time you take your dog out for a walk, an activity she loves very much, you put her leash on her. Now, whenever she sees you pick up the leash, your dog becomes excited, wags her tail, and runs to the door.

   UCS: _____   UCR: _____

   CS: _____   CR: _____

2. Bonnie loved to visit her favorite grandfather and was always sad when she had to leave him to go home. When she hugged him goodbye, he was always chewing Juicy Fruit gum. Today she feels a little down whenever she smells Juicy Fruit gum.

   UCS: _____   UCR: _____

   CS: _____   CR: _____

Expanding Your Knowledge and Understanding:
Name That Process

Processes in classical conditioning include acquisition, extinction, spontaneous recovery, generalization, and discrimination. Indicate which of these processes is described in each item.

1. Brooke loved cats until she was scratched by her neighbor's Siamese cat. Then she became scared whenever she saw any cat.

   _____

2. Rebecca quit eating chocolate a year ago and reports that for at least the last six months, she has had no cravings for chocolate whenever she saw or smelled it.

   _____

3. When you adopted your cat from the local animal shelter, she seemed very afraid of all people and hid whenever you or any person walked into the room. With time, your cat became comfortable around you but would still hide if any other person entered the room.

_____

4. Megan is very scared whenever there is a loud thunderstorm and she hides under her bed. When her father dropped a stack of dishes on the floor, Megan became afraid and ran to hide under her bed.

_____

5. Tom quit smoking a year ago and has had no desire for a cigarette for six months. However, last weekend he attended a party and a friend offered him a cigarette. Ever since that night, he has been craving a cigarette.

_____

Testing Your Knowledge and Understanding:
Multiple Choice Questions

1. Which of the following is not a fundamental feature of the definition of learning?
   a. experience
   b. relatively permanent
   c. change in behavior
   d. application of reinforcement

2. Which of the following is not an example of generalization in classical conditioning?
   a. Afraid of thunder, Christine jumps when she hears a firecracker.
   b. Afraid of lightning, Carrie learns to be afraid of the teddy bear she was holding when she last saw lightning.
   c. Afraid of dental drills, Melanie jumps when she hears a carpenter use an electric saw.
   d. Afraid of snakes, Tim jumps when he sees a rope in the grass.

3. Learning is a change in behavior caused by
   a. maturation
   b. motivation
   c. preparedness
   d. experience

4. Since his painful root canal, Jimmy cringes any time he hears a dentist's drill. Last week, remodeling on his house was started. Working at home, Jimmy continuously heard the sounds of drills, electric screwdrivers, and electric saws. After six days of this, Jimmy visits his dentist and is surprised to discover that the sound of the dentist drill did not bother him. What accounts for this new response?
   a. generalization
   b. acquisition
   c. extinction
   d. reflexive responses rule

5. Your piano teacher terrorized you during your lessons, striking your hands with a ruler when you played the wrong notes and being very critical of your playing. Your new boss looks just like your piano teacher, and you find that every time your boss looks at you, you are fearful. This response to your boss is an example of
   a. spontaneous recovery
   b. discrimination
   c. generalization
   d. extinction

6. Which of the following is an example of an unconditioned response?
   a. reading a book
   b. blinking when a puff of air hits your eye
   c. swimming in a pool
   d. laughing at a joke

7. Which is the correct sequence of classical conditioning processes?
   a. spontaneous recovery, acquisition, extinction
   b. extinction, spontaneous recovery, acquisition
   c. extinction, acquisition, spontaneous recovery
   d. acquisition, extinction, spontaneous recovery

ANSWERS

Name That Element

1. UCS: going outside
   UCR: excitement
   CS: leash
   CR: excitement

2. UCS: hugging and saying goodbye
   UCR: sadness
   CS: smell of Juicy Fruit gum
   CR: sadness

Name That Process

1. generalization
2. extinction
3. discrimination
4. generalization
5. spontaneous recovery

Multiple Choice

1. d
2. b
3. d
4. c
5. c
6. b
7. d

Chapter 13 -- Reward Has Powerful, Predictable Effects on Behavior

(or How Obnoxious Children Get That Way)

Checking Your Knowledge:
Terms, Statements, & Questions

After you have read this chapter, you should be able to define the terms/concepts, explain the statements, and answer the questions in this section *in your own words*. When appropriate, it may help to give a concrete example of the term or statement. It is most helpful if you try to answer in your own words before looking in the textbook.

1. cumulative response curve _____

_____

2. fixed interval schedule _____

_____

3. fixed ratio schedule _____

_____

4. negative reinforcer _____

_____

5. operant conditioning _____

_____

6. positive reinforcer _____

_____

7. variable interval schedule _____

_____

8. variable ratio schedule _____

_____

9. In operant conditioning, there is a contingency between a response and a reinforcer. _____

10. Operant rate is the frequency of a response when no response-reinforcer contingency exists.

_____

_____

11. A positive reinforcer is a contingent stimulus whose presentation is followed by an increase in
the rate of the particular behavior. _____

_____

_____

12. Primary reinforcers are stimuli that satisfy biological needs and are inherently reinforcing.

_____

_____

13. Secondary reinforcers are stimuli or events that acquire reinforcing properties. _____

_____

_____

14. Operant conditioning includes the processes of (a) generalization _____

_____

_____

    (b) discrimination _____

_____

    (c) extinction _____

_____

    . and (d) spontaneous recovery _____

_____

15. A discriminative stimulus is a stimulus whose presence indicates that reinforcement is possible and whose absence indicates that reinforcement is not possible. _____

_____

_____

16. Reinforcement can be (a) continuous _____

_____

_____

    or (b) partial _____

_____

_____

17. Partial reinforcement can be based on (a) an interval schedule _____

_____

_____

    or (b) a ratio schedule _____

_____

_____

18. Interval and ratio schedules can be (a) fixed _____

_____

_____

    or (b) variable _____

_____

_____

19. Why are money and attention considered secondary reinforcers? _____

_____

20. In the example given in the text about Rosie and her dad at the grocery store, explain each of the reinforcers involved. What kind are they (positive, negative, primary, secondary)? What behavior is each reinforcing? _____

_____

_____

_____

_____

Expanding Your Knowledge and Understanding: What Type of Reinforcer?

For each of the items below, indicate whether the behavior is being positively or negatively reinforced.

_____ 1. Tim is thanked for opening the door for his mother.

_____ 2. Sophie's mother stops nagging when Sophie empties the dishwasher.

_____ 3. Ryan turns off the alarm at 6 a.m. and jumps into the shower.

_____ 4. Brad listens to a new cd only after he studies for one hour.

Expanding Your Knowledge and Understanding: What Type of Schedule?

For each item, indicate if the schedule of reinforcement being used is continuous (C), fixed ratio (FR), variable ratio (VR), fixed interval (FI), or variable interval (VI).

_____ 1. receiving a paycheck every two weeks

_____ 2. getting $20 each time you mow the lawn

_____ 3. getting grades every 6 weeks

_____ 4. having pop quizzes in class to get students to study

_____ 5. getting paid once a week for weeding the garden

_____ 6. receiving a bonus for each third car sold by a car salesperson

_____ 7. receiving a balloon for each book a 7-year-old reads

_____ 8. playing a slot machine

_____ 9. being paid after every 10th cap you knit

_____ 10. selling Girl Scout cookies door-to-door

Testing Your Knowledge and Understanding: Multiple Choice Questions

1. What characteristic do positive reinforcement and negative reinforcement share?
    a. both involve the presentation of a stimulus
    b. both involve the removal of a stimulus
    c. both increase the rate at which a response occurs
    d. both decrease the rate at which a response occurs

2. Dr. Lewis tells her class that monthly tests will cover reading assignments from journal articles held on reserve at the library as well as information presented in the lectures. However, the first two tests contained only questions from the reading assignments. So students stopped taking notes during the lectures. Dr. Lewis has _____ note-taking behavior and _____ reading behavior.
    a. negatively reinforced; positively reinforced
    b. extinguished; negatively reinforced
    c. extinguished; positively reinforced
    d. positively reinforced; negatively reinforced

3. Which of the following suggests that Wayne's room-cleaning behavior is controlled by a discriminative stimulus?
   a. He cleans his room only when his mother--who gives him his allowance--is in town.
   b. He cleans his room whether his mother--who gives him his allowance--is in town or not.
   c. He cleans his room every week or so.
   d. He refuses to clean his room regardless of his mother's request.

4. With regard to schedule of reinforcement, number of responses is to period of time as _____ is to _____.
   a. interval; ratio
   b. ratio; interval
   c. variable; fixed
   d. fixed; variable

5. Which student does not understand operant conditioning?
   a. John: "Essentially all animal species find food and water as reinforcing."
   b. Michael: "An operant behavior is under the control of both a discriminative stimulus and the reinforcer."
   c. Eric: "Extinction is most likely to occur when a person has been reinforced only part of the time."
   d. Carol: "Operant conditioning involves learning an association between a behavior and its consequence."

6. Which of the following would be a negative reinforcer for most people?
   a. winning a new car
   b. flunking out of college
   c. having a serious traffic accident
   d. having an obnoxious noise stopped

7. Joel gets $10 for every 5 shirts he irons. He is on a _____ schedule.
   a. variable ratio
   b. variable interval
   c. fixed interval
   d. fixed ratio

Applying Your Knowledge and Understanding: Challenge

What two processes are associated with both classical conditioning and operant conditioning and have contributed to our learning and improved our adaptability as a species? How do the processes do that?

_____

_____

_____

_____

_____

_____

ANSWERS

What Type of Reinforcer?

1. positive
2. negative
3. negative
4. positive

What Type of Schedule?

1. fixed interval
2. continuous
3. fixed interval
4. variable interval
5. fixed interval
6. fixed ratio
7. continuous
8. variable ratio
9. fixed ratio
10. variable ratio

Multiple Choice

1. c
2. c
3. a
4. b
5. c
6. d
7. d

Challenge

Discrimination and generalization

Chapter 14 -- Punishment Has Powerful, Often Unpredictable Effects on Behavior

(or Why People Who Are Punished for Doing Bad Things Don't Always Stop Doing Them)

Checking Your Knowledge: Terms, Statements, & Questions

After you have read this chapter, you should be able to define the terms/concepts, explain the statements, and answer the questions in this section *in your own words*. When appropriate, it may help to give a concrete example of the term or statement. It is most helpful if you try to answer in your own words before looking in the textbook.

1. modeling _____

_____

2. negative feedback loop _____

_____

3. positive feedback loop _____

_____

4. punishment _____

_____

5. regression to the mean _____

_____

6. The goal of punishment is to decrease behavior. _____

_____

7. Consistency is an important factor in the effectiveness of punishment. _____

_____

_____

8. Speed of delivery is an important factor in the effectiveness of punishment. _____

_____

9. Punishment may suppress a response only temporarily. _____

_____

_____

10. Punishment may suppress a response only in particular contexts. _____

_____

_____

11. The punisher may be feared by the organism receiving the punishment. _____

_____

_____

12. Punishment may generalize to other behaviors and/or situations. _____

_____

_____

13. What are the differences between punishment, positive reinforcement, and negative

reinforcement? _____

_____

_____

14. How can punishment work vicariously? _____

_____

_____

15. Why are both learning (operant conditioning) and the effects of punishment slower when the

reinforcement/punishment is not delivered consistently after each instance of the behavior?

_____

_____

_____

_____

16. What do the authors say are unintended consequences of punishment? Can you think of any

others? _____

_____

_____

_____

17. What are the side effects of delivering punishment? _____

_____

_____

_____

Expanding Your Knowledge and Understanding: Which Is It?

Indicate whether the examples below involve punishment, positive reinforcement, or negative reinforcement.

_____   1. Chris is issued a $100 speeding ticket.

_____   2. JoAnn is charged $25 for bouncing a check.

_____   3. Patti takes an aspirin for her splitting headache.

_____   4. Andrea studies hard for her next test to avoid getting another F.

_____   5. When Smoky the cat jumps up on the kitchen table, he is "shot" with a water pistol.

_____   6. Brandon is allowed to watch TV when he finishes his homework.

_____   7. Ashley cleans her room to avoid having to clean the garage too.

95

_____   8. When Adam breaks curfew, his parents ground him.

_____   9. When Abbey stays in her chair during reading hour, Ms. Johnson lets her stand in the front of the line going out for recess.

_____   10. A hockey player is placed in the penalty box for "high sticking" his opponent.

_____   11. Mike's license was suspended for drunk driving.

_____   12. Kristen smiles each time Brad makes a funny face.

_____   13. Sandy's professor screamed, "Stop snoring, sleepy head!" when she fell asleep in class.

_____   14. Becky is scolded for throwing rocks at passing cars.

_____   15. Laura buckles her seat belt in order to turn off the seat belt buzzer.

Testing Your Knowledge and Understanding: Multiple Choice Questions

1. Both negative reinforcement and punishment
   a. weaken behaviors they follow
   b. involve presenting an aversive stimulus
   c. are operant contingencies
   d. strengthen the behaviors they follow

2. Which student does not understand punishment?
   a. Jean: "In the short term, punishment can produce a decreased rate of behavior."
   b. Jim: "In the presence of the punisher, punishment can produce a decreased rate of behavior."
   c. Tom: "Timing is crucial for punishment to work."
   d. Carly: "The punisher and punishee always know which behavior is being punished."

3. According to Dr. Thomas, "Punishment is a behavioral consequence that is intended to decrease a behavior. On a temporary basis, such suppression may be possible. Moreover, it can be used to teach adaptive behavior. However, punishment can make a person more hostile or aggressive." Which statement is wrong?
   a. Punishment is a behavioral consequence that is intended to decrease a behavior.
   b. On a temporary basis, such suppression may be possible when punishment is used.
   c. Punishment can be used to teach adaptive behavior.
   d. Punishment can make a person more hostile or aggressive.

4. Who understood the difference between punishment and negative reinforcement?
   a. John: "Both involve the presentation of an aversive stimulus."
   b. William: "In punishment, a stimulus is turned on after a response and in negative reinforcement, a stimulus is turned off after the response."
   c. Claire: "In negative reinforcement, a positive stimulus is terminated and in punishment, a negative stimulus is terminated."
   d. Anna: "In negative reinforcement, a stimulus is turned on after a response and in punishment, a stimulus is turned off after a response."

5. To be effective, punishment should be
   a. administered after the person has time to think about the targeted behavior
   b. only for the most extreme level of a behavior
   c. at the lowest possible level -- after all, the level can be increased over time
   d. immediately and consistently

6. When Mike failed geometry, his parents took away his keys to the car. This consequence was a
   a. negative reinforcer
   b. punisher
   c. positive reinforcer
   d. controlled stimulus

7. A parent using punishment may find it habit-forming because stopping someone's unwanted behavior may _____ the punisher.
   a. positively reinforce
   b. generalize the pleasure for
   c. negatively reinforce
   d. upset

8. If parents used punishment frequently with their child, they may discover that
   a. they are producing generalized aggressiveness in their child
   b. they are successfully extinguishing all aggressiveness in their child
   c. they are raising a very obedient child
   d. their child will develop a severe personality disorder

Applying Your Knowledge and Understanding: Challenge

1. "Time-out" is a punishing consequence many parents use when their children misbehave. However, time-out has also been classified as a negative reinforcer and a positive reinforcer. Explain how a time-out can be

(a) punishment _____

_____

_____

_____

(b) negative reinforcement _____

_____

_____

_____

(c) positive reinforcement _____

_____

_____

_____

2. Sometimes a mother will tell a misbehaving child, "Just wait until your father comes home. Then you'll *really* get it." Which rules of thumb about the use of punishment are violated by this mother's behavior? What might be the unwanted consequences of such behavior?

_____

_____

_____

_____

ANSWERS

Which Is It?

1. punishment
2. punishment
3. negative reinforcement
4. negative reinforcement
5. punishment
6. positive reinforcement
7. negative reinforcement
8. punishment

9. positive reinforcement
10. punishment
11. punishment
12. positive reinforcement
13. punishment
14. punishment
15. negative reinforcement

Multiple Choice

1. c
2. d
3. c
4. b

5. d
6. b
7. c
8. a

Chapter 15 -- Behavior Is Flexible, but It Isn't Infinitely Flexible

(or Why It's Hard to Teach a Pig to Use a Piggy Bank)

Checking Your Knowledge:
Terms, Statements, & Questions

After you have read this chapter, you should be able to define the terms/concepts, explain the statements, and answer the questions in this section *in your own words*. When appropriate, it may help to give a concrete example of the term or statement. It is most helpful if you try to answer in your own words before looking in the textbook.

1. behaviorism

2. classical conditioning

3. instinctive drift

4. operant conditioning

5. prepared learning

6. Response acquisition via positive and negative reinforcement is similar in virtually all species of animals. _____

7. The termination of reinforcement results in extinction in virtually all species of animals. _____

8. Greater resistance to extinction following partial reinforcement is similar in virtually all species of animals. _____

_____

_____

9. Instinctive drift limits the generalization of basic operant conditioning effects. _____

_____

_____

_____

10. Prepared learning makes some operant responses easier to condition than others. _____

_____

_____

_____

11. What is a conditioned taste aversion? Why is it (evolutionarily) fitness-enhancing? _____

_____

_____

_____

12. In Garcia's study of the effects of radiation in rats, why did the rats avoid the water in their radiation chambers, but not in their home cages? _____

_____

_____

_____

Expanding Your Knowledge and Understanding: Phobias

People can develop a phobia to essentially any object. However, phobias to some objects are much more common than to other objects. For example, fears of heights, darkness, and snakes are more common while fears of television or three-legged stools are comparatively less common.

1. How can you explain this observation? _____

_____

_____

_____

2. What characteristics do these commonly phobic objects share that are not seen in objects of

uncommon phobias? _____

_____

_____

_____

3. During a thunderstorm, why might a child develop a fear of lightning, but not of rain or dark

clouds? _____

_____

_____

_____

4. How is this observation related to the evolution of the species? _____

_____

_____

Testing Your Knowledge and Understanding:
Multiple Choice Questions

1. What is instinctive drift?
   a. the importance of conditioning instincts in domesticated animals
   b. the ease with which animals learn instincts
   c. the natural generalization of responses across situations
   d. the tendency for an animal's innate response to interfere with conditioning

2. In response to a question about the limitations of the effectiveness of operant conditioning techniques, students wrote the following responses. Who failed this question?
   a. Amanda: "Essentially any response can be conditioned."
   b. Emily: "If an animal has prepared learning for a particular behavior, then operant conditioning techniques will be powerful."
   c. Sarah: "If an animal is contra-prepared to learn a particular behavior, then the application of operant conditioning techniques will be diminished."
   d. Rhonda: "The laws of operant conditioning generalize quite a lot, but not across all behaviors and species."

3. _____ is when an animal's response tendencies interfere with the conditioning process.
   a. Prepared learning
   b. Instinctive drift
   c. Inappropriate learning
   d. Instinctive aversion

4. Which student has the best understanding of the instinctive drift predispositions in conditioning?
   a. Hope: "Research to support the existence of instinctive predispositions is mixed, so any conclusions are premature."
   b. Bob: "Non-human organisms have instinctive predispositions that impact conditioning but human brains are so developed that they have lost such predispositions."
   c. Meredith: "Instinctive predispositions favor conditioning involving visual or auditory stimuli and make olfactory and taste stimuli more difficult to use."
   d. Bette: "Not all stimuli are created equal -- some associations are easier to learn while others are harder, if not essentially impossible."

5. A new animal trainer was convinced that he was "born" to train animals when he was able to train a raccoon to wash a plate in a stream. But when he tried unsuccessfully to teach a pig to do the same thing, he questioned if he was in the right profession. The problem is that he failed to consider
   a. the importance of observational learning
   b. the limitations of reinforcement
   c. the contribution of instinctive drift
   d. the value of negative reinforcement

6. Which of the following chemotherapy patients would you expect to be most likely to develop a conditioned taste aversion?
   a. a young child
   b. a person who eats at least five favorite foods five hours before a chemotherapy session
   c. a person who eats an unusual new food three hours before a chemotherapy session
   d. a person who eats no food during the five hours before a chemotherapy session

Applying Your Knowledge and Understanding: Challenge

Dr. Jennings escorted his wife on a "night on the town" for their 25th wedding anniversary. He had planned a very romantic evening, beginning with an expensive dinner at an exclusive restaurant. After dinner, they were going to see a Broadway show.

At dinner, Dr. Jennings ordered oysters and he and his wife enjoyed every bite. However, about 3 a.m. the next morning, Dr. Jennings awoke with intense stomach cramps and he spent the next several hours vomiting. After that night, the mere thought of oysters caused Dr. Jennings to turn green, become nauseous, and look for the closest bathroom.

1. What has occurred? _____

_____

2. What type of conditioning is involved? _____

_____

3. Identify the basic elements involved in this conditioning episode. _____

_____

_____

_____

_____

4. What basic principles of conditioning are violated by this example? _____

_____

_____

_____

_____

ANSWERS

Multiple Choice

1. d
2. a
3. b
4. d
5. c
6. c

Chapter 16 -- Television Has Substantial Negative Effects on Beliefs and Behavior

(or Why It's Better for Kids to Watch PBS Than Network TV)

Checking Your Knowledge:
Terms, Statements, & Questions

After you have read this chapter, you should be able to define the terms/concepts, explain the statements, and answer the questions in this section *in your own words*. When appropriate, it may help to give a concrete example of the term or statement. It is most helpful if you try to answer in your own words before looking in the textbook.

1. observational learning _____

_____

2. Learning can occur vicariously. _____

_____

_____

3. Exposure to TV violence causes increases in aggressive behavior, but it is not the only cause of

aggressive behavior. _____

_____

_____

4. Was the Williams and Handford study examining TV viewing habits in three Canadian towns a

true experimental design? Why or why not? _____

_____

_____

5. In the Bandura, Ross, and Ross study on modeling behavior, (a) what did the children who

witnessed an adult get punished for aggressive behavior do when they were in the room with

the doll? _____

_____

_____

(b) What did they do when the experimenter asked them to demonstrate what they had seen, telling them they wouldn't be punished for it? _____

_____

_____

(c) How do you explain the difference in behaviors? _____

_____

_____

6. What is the general conclusion about the effects of TV violence on aggression? What are some of the problems with research in this area? _____

_____

_____

_____

7. What did you learn in Part 4 (chapters 12, 13, 14, 15, and 16) that supports the Basic Idea that "*much* human behavior results from an interaction between past experience and the immediate situation?" _____

_____

_____

_____

8. What did you learn in Part 4 that supports the Basic Idea that "adaptation is *the* fundamental property of human behavior and cognition?" _____

_____

_____

9. What did you learn in Part 4 to support the Basic Idea that "you cannot understand psychology without understanding evolution. Behavior results from an interaction between genetic factors and the immediate situation?" _____

_____

_____

_____

_____

Expanding Your Knowledge and Understanding: Violence Exposure

1. Given that the average person sees as many as 3,000 violent acts each year watching TV, do people habituate to the violence on TV? If not, what factors do you think prohibit such habituation?

_____

_____

_____

_____

_____

2. Does viewing so much violence on TV desensitize people to the consequences of violence? Are there ways to prevent such desensitization?

_____

_____

_____

_____

_____

3. What personal characteristics may interact with the viewing of violence on television? Are there groups of children who may be particularly affected by viewing violence on TV?

_____

_____

_____

_____

4. Do you think altruistic (helping) behavior could be learned vicariously? If so, in what ways?

_____

_____

_____

_____

_____

Testing Your Knowledge and Understanding:
Multiple Choice Questions

1. In observational learning
   a. an individual is reinforced for being observed
   b. an individual is reinforced for watching a model
   c. an individual's behavior is influenced by watching others
   d. an individual learns to associate an observed behavior with a neutral stimulus

2. Reinforcement determines the _____ of a behavior in operant conditioning and the _____ of a behavior in observational learning.
   a. learning; performance
   b. learning; learning
   c. performance; learning
   d. performance; performance

3. Tommy sees his father hit his mother regularly whenever his father is angry. When Tommy plays with the little girl next door and he gets angry, he is likely to
   a. hit the little girl
   b. hit his mother
   c. hit himself
   d. cry

4. Which student has the wrong understanding of observational learning?
   a. Joy: "Most complex behaviors of humans are learned through observational learning."
   b. Whitney: "Trial and error is the initial phase of observational learning."
   c. Adam: "A person may learn a behavior but not perform it."
   d. Troy: "Operant learning can take place vicariously through observational learning."

5. Sheila and Todd watched "Superman" on TV. Afterwards, their parents found them jumping off the dog's house trying to fly. Sheila and Todd are manifesting
   a. classical conditioning
   b. entertainment learning
   c. reinforced learning
   d. observational learning

Applying Your Knowledge and Understanding: Challenge

A concern of some parents and psychologists is the amount of violence in many computer games. Design a study that would address the question "Do computer games involving violence increase the player's level of aggression?"

Participants: _____

_____

Experimental group: _____

_____

Control group: _____

_____

Independent variable: _____

_____

Dependent variable: _____

_____

Procedure: _____

_____

_____

_____

Expected findings: _____

_____

_____

_____

ANSWERS

Multiple Choice

1. c
2. a
3. a
4. b
5. d

Chapter 17 -- Working Memory Is Involved in Many Cognitive Activities, but Has a Very Limited Capacity

(or Why Telephone Numbers That Include the Area Code Are Hard to Remember)

Checking Your Knowledge:
Terms, Statements, & Questions

After you have read this chapter, you should be able to define the terms/concepts, explain the statements, and answer the questions in this section *in your own words*. When appropriate, it may help to give a concrete example of the term or statement. It is most helpful if you try to answer in your own words before looking in the textbook.

1. acoustic coding _____

_____

2. chunking _____

_____

3. elaborative rehearsal _____

_____

4. encoding _____

_____

5. executive _____

_____

6. maintenance rehearsal _____

_____

7. mnemonics _____

_____

8. primacy effect _____

_____

9. retrieval

_____

_____

10. recency effect

_____

_____

11. sensory memory

_____

_____

12. working memory

_____

_____

13. Sequenced actions require working memory. _____

_____

14. Problem solving requires working memory. _____

_____

15. Planning and decision making require working memory. _____

_____

16. Language comprehension requires working memory. _____

_____

17. Working memory has a very limited capacity. _____

_____

18. Information in working memory may come from the environment or from long-term memory.

_____

_____

19. Much of the encoding in working memory uses some form of acoustic code; however, other

forms of material can be encoded and maintained in working memory. _____

_____

20. Decay and displacement are possible explanations for the loss of information from working memory. _____

_____

21. Verbal material is maintained in part through maintenance rehearsal and elaborative rehearsal.

_____

_____

22. Retrieval of information from working memory is automatic. _____

_____

_____

23. How is information stored in working memory? _____

_____

_____

_____

24. How is information retrieved from working memory? _____

_____

_____

_____

Expanding Your Knowledge and Understanding: The Memory Model

In what part of the memory model are each of the following pieces of information likely to be found -- long-term memory, working memory, or sensory memory?

_____   1. what you ate for breakfast yesterday

_____   2. this "word" right now

_____   3. the first part of a sentence your instructor just finished speaking

_____   4. the zip code you just looked up

_____   5. how to spell "exceptionally"

_____   6. the smell of the cookies your grandmother used to bake

_____   7. the name of your first grade teacher

_____   8. the phone number for the new pizza place you just looked up in the phone book

_____   9. the date of your brother's birthday

_____   10. the unit price of a box of cereal that you just figured out in your head in order to compare the price to another brand at the grocery store

Testing Your Knowledge and Understanding: Multiple Choice Questions

1. Material is maintained in working memory for about
   a. 60 minutes
   b. 1 minute
   c. 15-20 seconds
   d. 15-20 minutes

2. Edith's work number is 202-555-4357, extension 5263. Since she has difficulty remembering all of these numbers at once, she remembers the number as "two hundred and two, five hundred and fifty-five, forty-three, fifty-seven, fifty-two, sixty-three." She is using _____ to help her remember the number.
   a. cuing
   b. chunking
   c. categories
   d. mnemonics

3. The order of getting information into working memory is
   a. sensory memory, environment, attention, encoding
   b. environment, attention, sensory memory, encoding
   c. sensory memory, attention, executive, working memory
   d. environment, sensory memory, attention, working memory

4. Which of the following is not an example of evidence for acoustic encoding?
   a. encoding according to how an item looks
   b. encoding according to how an item sounds
   c. fewer items are recalled when the items sound alike
   d. the making of intrusion errors

5. Which of the following is not an intrusion error?
   a. remembering a T as a C
   b. remembering a word that sounds like the word to be remembered
   c. remembering a B as an E
   d. remembering a Q as an O

6. Students offered the following descriptions of working memory. Who doesn't understand working memory?
   a. Anna: "There is evidence for visual coding in working memory."
   b. Hillary: "The acoustic store and visual/spatial store are independent of one another."
   c. Kenneth: "Working memory is involved in comprehension of language."
   d. Daniel: "With intense practice, the capacity of working memory can be increased."

7. Which of the following is not a way in which working memory is involved in language comprehension?
   a. It is necessary for remembering what was already said in previous conversations.
   b. It is required for the comprehension of complex sentences.
   c. Working memory provides the context for understanding complex discourse.
   d. Working memory is necessary to retain the beginning of a sentence for when the sentence is completed.

8. The capacity of _____ is _____.
   a. working memory; large
   b. sensory memory; small
   c. long-term memory; huge
   d. buffer; very large

9. The capacity of working memory is about _____ pieces of information for _____.
    a. 2; 45 seconds
    b. 9; 35 seconds
    c. 7; 20 seconds
    d. 5; 5 seconds

10. As you parked your car at the mall on a very busy shopping day, you glanced at the cars on either side of your car. However, when you are asked to recall the colors of those cars, you are unable to do so because
    a. your sensory memory lasts only 15 minutes
    b. information is not encoded into working memory unless attention is paid to the information
    c. this information was displaced by information you processed while shopping
    d. the information was lost in long-term memory

11. A long list of unrelated words including the word "cat" was read to Emma. When she was asked to recall as many of the words as possible, she erroneously included "chat" as one of the words. This is an example of
    a. an intrusion error
    b. visual encoding
    c. memory decay
    d. a hedonic error

Applying Your Knowledge and Understanding: Challenge

Note: This exercise should be spaced over a number of days.

Volunteering with the Red Cross, you are preparing to serve as a disaster worker following a flood. As you plan to pack, you review the list of things you are recommended to bring. The list is:

clothes for 10 days
a radio
a blank check
closed-toe shoes
reading book
black-ink pens
glasses
written policies
name tag
Red Cross t-shirts
work gloves
shampoo

blank forms
money
batteries
hand soap
battery-operated alarm clock
camera
one set of dress clothes
Red Cross vest
toothbrush/toothpaste
informational handouts
medicine
Red Cross identification card

insurance card
cap or hat
driver's license
film
clipboard
sunglasses

Day 1: After reading the list, cover it up and write down all of the items you remember. How many did you remember?   _____

Day 2: How could you use chunking to help you remember these items? After you have developed a chunking approach, how concepts did you remember?   _____

Day 3: How could you use mnemonics to help you remember the items? After you have developed a mnemonic device, how many items could you remember?   _____

Day 4: How many items can you remember using maintenance rehearsal?   _____

Day 5: How many items can you remember using elaborative rehearsal?   _____

How did the various methods help you in remembering items from the list? Did any of the items get encoded into your long-term memory as a function of using these different encoding methods? In other words, did you find that you still remembered some items at the beginning of a new day as a result of doing this exercise the day before (or two or three days before)?

_____

_____

_____

_____

ANSWERS

The Memory Model

1. long-term
2. sensory
3. working
4. working
5. long-term
6. long-term
7. long-term
8. working
9. long-term
10. working

Multiple Choice

1. c
2. b
3. d
4. a
5. d
6. d
7. a
8. c
9. c
10. b
11. a

Chapter 18 -- Long-Term Memory Is Vast, Powerful, and Fallible

*(or How You Know Who You Are, Where You Are,
and Where You're Going--Most of the Time)*

Checking Your Knowledge:
Terms, Statements, & Questions

After you have read this chapter, you should be able to define the terms/concepts, explain the statements, and answer the questions in this section *in your own words*. When appropriate, it may help to give a concrete example of the term or statement. It is most helpful if you try to answer in your own words before looking in the textbook.

1. flash-bulb memory _____

    _____

2. long-term memory _____

    _____

3. method of loci _____

    _____

4. mnemonics _____

    _____

5. representations _____

    _____

6. simplification _____

    _____

7. Flash-bulb memories may not be accurate. _____

    _____

8. The capacity of long-term memory has no known limitations but not every event is in an

    individual's memory and/or is retrievable. _____

    _____

9. Memories are determined by both actual events and constructive mental processes. _____

_____

_____

10. Simplifying and organizing memories has the cost of producing memories that are not

"perfectly accurate." _____

_____

11. Three memory processes are: (a) encoding _____

_____

    (b) storage _____

_____

    and (c) retrieval _____

_____

12. The majority of encoding and storage in long-term memory is semantic. _____

_____

_____

13. The deliberate use of retrieval cues during the encoding of information facilitates retrieval.

_____

_____

14. Working memory and long-term memory are separate systems located in different parts of the

brain. What is the evidence for this? _____

_____

_____

_____

15. How good are we at remembering other people? _____

_____

    places? _____

_____

    language? _____

_____

    mathematics? _____

_____

    Summarize the results of Bahrick's research in these areas. _____

_____

_____

_____

16. What does it mean to say that memory is a constructive, active process? _____

_____

_____

17. In the Loftus and Palmer study on eyewitness testimony, why did subjects who were asked how fast the cars were going when they "smashed into" each other recall higher speeds and more broken glass than other subjects did? _____

_____

_____

_____

_____

Expanding Your Knowledge and Understanding:
Which Memory Aid?

1. In this chapter and the last, several memory aids (e.g., maintenance rehearsal, chunking, elaborative rehearsal, mnemonics, and methods of loci) have been introduced. These aids are not interchangeable; rather, their use is appropriate in different situations. Which memory aids do you think would be most effective for the following memory tasks?

    _____ A. remembering a seldom-used telephone number
    that you just looked up in the phone book

    _____ B. remembering your grocery shopping list

    _____ C. as a waiter, remembering the orders for a table of five

    _____ D. remembering the names of the bones in your hand

    _____ E. remembering the notes on a treble clef

2. What is the pattern in the use of these memory aids? Do you notice a difference in which memory aids are most helpful based on whether the items to be remembered are going into working memory or long-term memory?

    _____

    _____

    _____

    _____

    _____

Testing Your Knowledge and Understanding:
Multiple Choice Questions

1. Your visual memory of your dog sleeping when you left for school this morning is stored in your
   a. sensory memory
   b. buffer
   c. working memory
   d. long-term memory

2. _____ are memories of events that are highly significant and vividly remembered.
   a. Eyewitness sensations
   b. Flash-bulb memories
   c. Immediate sensations
   d. Critical memories

3. Eyewitness testimony
   a. is not likely to be perfectly accurate
   b. is restricted to sensory memory
   c. remains in working memory
   d. cannot be encoded into long-term memory

4. Ken's fiance has 10 brothers and sisters. Ken is worried about getting their names when he meets them, so his visualizes them in a particular way. For example, Ann is in a pan and Steve has dirty sleeves from cleaning the stove. He is using
   a. method of loci
   b. a mnemonic technique
   c. maintenance rehearsal
   d. poetic meaning

5. Autobiographical memories
   a. are easily recalled from the perspective of the person who has the original experience
   b. are most often from the perspective of an observer
   c. are maintained in sensory memory
   d. go directly from sensory memory to long-term memory

6. As a member of a jury -- but one who has taken General Psychology -- you should know that eyewitness testimony
   a. is true -- after all, the witness was there and you were not
   b. is invalid and can never be trusted
   c. is always subject to representation and simplification
   d. can be trusted only if it has remained in working memory

7. When retrieving information, the amount recalled will be greater if the conditions under which retrieval is attempted are _____ those in which encoding was done.
   a. very different from
   b. very similar to
   c. simpler than
   d. more complex than

8. Brenna regularly misspells "psychology," so she uses the following sentence to help her remember: "Paul Sees Young Chickens Hollow Out Logs On Green Yards." Brenna is employing
   a. the method of loci
   b. elaborative rehearsal
   c. a mnemonic device
   d. dissociation

Applying Your Knowledge and Understanding: Challenge

When an individual's hippocampus is destroyed, that person is unable to transfer information from working memory to long-term memory. The individual would be able to retrieve memories already stored in long-term memory. For example, the person would remember his or her name, occupation, family members (prior to injury), how to write, talk, walk, play cards, and any other facts or activities that were learned prior to the injury. However, no new memories would be encoded in long-term memory. No matter how many times a person practiced a new activity or was told the name of a new family member, the information would not be encoded.

1. Think of a typical day in your life. How would such hippocampal damage impact even one activity (e.g., eating meals, taking medicine, picking up your kids at school) on that typical day?

   _____

   _____

   _____

   _____

   _____

   _____

2. What steps could you take to help you complete your routine daily activities as best as you could with hippocampal damage? (Remember that no matter what memory aids you may attempt, the information will not be encoded into your long-term memory.)

_____

_____

_____

_____

_____

_____

ANSWERS

Which Memory Aid?

1. A. chunking or maintenance rehearsal
    B. mnemonics or elaborative rehearsal
    C. chunking or method of loci
    D. mnemonics or elaborative rehearsal
    E. mnemonics or elaborative rehearsal

2. Chunking and maintenance rehearsal are memory aids for working memory and mnemonic devices and elaborative rehearsal are memory aids primarily for long-term memory.

Multiple Choice

1. d   5. b
2. b   6. c
3. a   7. b
4. b   8. c

Chapter 19 -- The More You Know the Easier It Is to Learn New Things

(or How to Master the Material in This, and Most Other, Books)

Checking Your Knowledge:
Terms, Statements, & Questions

After you have read this chapter, you should be able to define the terms/concepts, explain the statements, and answer the questions in this section *in your own words*. When appropriate, it may help to give a concrete example of the term or statement. It is most helpful if you try to answer in your own words before looking in the textbook.

1. schema _____

_____

2. script _____

_____

3. Prior learning affects later learning. _____

_____

_____

4. Schemas are interconnected sets of information that are involved in the processing and retention

of new material. _____

_____

_____

5. A script is a particular type of schema that tells us how to act in certain situations. _____

_____

_____

6. What is the difference between lower-order skills and higher-order skills? _____

_____

_____

7. Why do lower-order skills need to be mastered in order to facilitate mastery of higher-order skills? _____

_____

_____

8. What did you learn in Part 5 (chapters 17, 18, and 19) that supports the Basic Idea that "adaptation is *the* fundamental property of human behavior and cognition?" _____

_____

_____

_____

9. What did you learn in Part 5 that supports the Basic Idea that "memory is active, not passive. We *construct* internal representations of the past, but don't just make them up?" _____

_____

_____

_____

10. What did you learn in Part 5 that supports the Basic Idea that "humans have the ability to think and reason in *very* powerful ways, but we also have a number of cognitive limitations that lead to systematic errors?" _____

_____

_____

_____

11. What did you learn in Part 5 that supports the Basic Idea that "many cognitive limitations can be overcome by using cognitive tools?" _____

_____

_____

Expanding Your Knowledge and Understanding:
Teaching to Foster Learning

After reading this chapter, critique your instructor's teaching style. Are there ways that your instructor could improve his or her lecture style to foster greater learning by you? (Note, the goal is to foster learning, not to get you out of class 20 minutes early each day...) Identify specific behaviors or changes.

_____

_____

_____

_____

_____

_____

_____

Testing Your Knowledge and Understanding:
Multiple Choice Questions

1. When asked to identify the function of schemas, students offered the following responses. Who did not understand this chapter?
    a. Raymond: "Schemas are knowledge-based frameworks."
    b. Deborah: "Schemas facilitate learning by providing a mental structure for organizing incoming information."
    c. Marie: "Schemas are also called frames."
    d. Robert: "Schemas form highly organized hierarchical networks that are independent of one another."

2. What is the relationship between old learning and the learning of new information?
    a. Old learning interferes with new learning if both learnings are similar in nature.
    b. New learning displaces old learning but only if the types of learning are independent of one another.
    c. New learning facilitates old learning.
    d. Old learning facilitates new learning.

3. Which of the following statements is false?
   a. Mastery of lower-order skills facilitates the mastery of higher-order skills.
   b. Mastery of lower-order skills fosters efficient learning and performance.
   c. Mastery of lower-order skills fosters efficient performance but interferes with new learning.
   d. Mastery of lower-order skills makes learning easier.

4. If students were asked to read a complex, untitled theme and to recall immediately as many facts included in them as they could, who would likely recall the most number of facts?
   a. a student who was not restricted by being told that the theme was about a particular topic
   b. a student who was told before reading the theme what it was about
   c. a student who was told after reading the theme what it was about
   d. it would make no difference

5. Expectations about how a college professor should behave in the class is a student's
   a. script
   b. schema
   c. model roles
   d. specific sequences

Applying Your Knowledge and Understanding: Challenges

1. Suggestions for improving learning in courses often includes the following:

   1. During lectures, give your complete attention.
   2. During lectures, try to anticipate what will be said next.
   3. During lectures, look for deeper meanings.
   4. Read the chapter before your professor lectures on it.
   5. Write your lecture notes in your own words.
   6. Ask questions during the lecture.

   How do these suggestions fit with the information presented in this chapter?

   _____

   _____

   _____

   _____

   _____

2. Knowing that learning is easier when you can incorporate the material into a framework, or schema, have the authors of the text given you any good ideas about how to learn the material in this particular book? If so, what are they? If so, have you implemented these ideas yet? If not, do you think they might help you?

_____

_____

_____

_____

_____

_____

ANSWERS

Multiple Choice

1. d
2. d
3. c
4. b
5. b

Chapter 20 -- Intuitive Judgments about Things Having to Do with Numbers Are Often Wrong

(or Why Millions of People Play the Lottery Every Week)

Checking Your Knowledge:
Terms, Statements, & Questions

After you have read this chapter, you should be able to define the terms/concepts, explain the statements, and answer the questions in this section *in your own words*. When appropriate, it may help to give a concrete example of the term or statement. It is most helpful if you try to answer in your own words before looking in the textbook.

1. availability heuristic   _____

_____

2. base rate   _____

_____

3. false alarm   _____

_____

4. heuristic   _____

_____

5. positive hit   _____

_____

6. representativeness
   heuristic   _____

_____

7. An algorithm is an exact method for determining the exact answer. _____

_____

_____

8. A heuristic is a "rule of thumb" for getting an approximately correct answer. _____

_____

9. Although heuristics generally work well, they are problematic if used in the wrong situation.

_____

_____

10. Reliance on heuristics may cause one to ignore other important information. _____

_____

_____

11. What are the advantages to using heuristics when making judgments about numbers? _____

_____

_____

_____

12. What are the disadvantages to using heuristics when making judgments about numbers? ____

_____

_____

_____

13. Why is it important to pay attention to how often the observed effect occurs in the absence of

the presumed cause when you are considering questions of causality? _____

_____

_____

_____

14. Why is it important to pay attention to base rates when you are considering questions of

causality? _____

_____

_____

Expanding Your Knowledge and Understanding:
Algorithms and Heuristics

1. The Lost Cat

Neil's cat, Freeway, is hiding somewhere in the house. Explain how Neil could look for him

(a) using an algorithm? _____

_____

_____

(b) using a heuristic? _____

_____

_____

2. Sisters and Brothers

You are about to meet a family with eight children -- four girls and four boys. Below are four possible birth orders for the children. Indicate the relative likelihood of each possibility by rank ordering them. Use a 1-4 scale, with 1 being the most likely.

Possible order	Likelihood rank
G G G G B B B B	_____
B G B G B G B G	_____
B B G G B B G G	_____
B B G B G G G B	_____

(a) What is the reasoning for your rank ordering? _____

_____

_____

_____

(b) What mistake do most people make in answering a question such as this? _____

_____

_____

_____

_____

3. IQ Scores

(a) If you were to assess the IQs of five people, which group of scores would you more likely obtain?

$$100 \quad 100 \quad 100 \quad 100 \quad 100 \qquad or \qquad 130 \quad 130 \quad 130 \quad 130 \quad 130$$

_____

_____

_____

(b) If you knew that the base rate for people with an IQ of 100 was much greater than the base rate for people with an IQ of 130, would your answer change?

_____

_____

_____

Testing Your Knowledge and Understanding: Multiple Choice Questions

1. If you want to guarantee a solution, the problem-solving methods you should use are
   a. algorithms
   b. trial and error
   c. experimental thinking
   d. heuristics

2. If you want a rule of thumb that offers an approximate answer, you would use
   a. algorithms
   b. trial and error
   c. successive approximation
   d. heuristics

3. Which student displays the best understanding of heuristics and algorithms?
   a. Casey: "When confronted with a problem, people use algorithms more often than heuristics."
   b. Dana: "Both produce answers, but only algorithms result in the exact answer."
   c. Jeremy: "Heuristics require more time to use than algorithms do."
   d. Natalie: "Algorithms require less time to use but provide the exact answer."

4. Which student needs to reread the chapter, if an A on the upcoming exam is expected?
   a. Dan: "Heuristics can be particularly helpful in problem solving because they are quick and easy."
   b. Sally: "The usefulness of a heuristic may be situation-specific."
   c. Isaac: "It is usually very difficult for people to use algorithms to solve complex problems in their heads."
   d. Kim: "Heuristics should be used only when an exact answer is required."

5. Five-year-old Donny is learning how to subtract. When facing the following problem, $\begin{array}{r} 21 \\ -14 \\ \hline \end{array}$
   he learns to "borrow 10 from the second column and add it to the first column..."
   He is learning
   a. an algorithm
   b. a heuristic
   c. representativeness
   d. the mathematica heuristic

6. Sam has been watching Leo flip a coin 25 times, getting heads each time. Sam bets that the next toss will be tails. His prediction is probably based on
   a. the availability heuristic
   b. the representativeness heuristic
   c. the availability algorithm
   d. the representativeness algorithm

7. Who is using the availability heuristic in determining the divorce rate?
   a. Donna goes to the library for the official statistics obtained in the U.S. Census.
   b. Toby conducts a survey in his hometown.
   c. Charlie thinks about how many of his friends are divorced.
   d. Josh decides that since you have a 50-50 chance of divorce, the rate is 50%.

8. Observing the never-ending activity of 4-year-old Aaron, Ms. Johnson, a nursery school teacher, is convinced that Aaron is hyperactive. His behavior is consistent with what she thinks hyperactivity is. Ms. Johnson's thinking demonstrates her use of
   a. base rates
   b. the availability heuristic
   c. the representativeness heuristic
   d. algorithms

9. Which of the following is an example of an instance where using the availability heuristic can lead you to the wrong answer?
   a. Estimating there are more trees in a lot than there actually are.
   b. Estimating the price of a new house after looking at other houses.
   c. Estimating that Harley Davidsons are the most frequently sold motorcycles since most of your biker friends own Harleys.
   d. Estimating that one of two pies is larger when one is farther away.

Applying Your Knowledge and Understanding: Challenge

How might the availability heuristic be used in the following situations? When would it be likely to lead to errors in judgment?

1. shopping for toothpaste _____

_____

_____

_____

2. people's perception of the dangers of certain diseases (e.g., cancer, diabetes) _____

_____

_____

_____

3. increasing self-confidence for a job interview _____

_____

_____

_____

4. a physician's decision to recommend a particularly dangerous medical procedure that has

been successful for his last 10 patients _____

_____

_____

_____

5. a physician's decision to recommend a particularly dangerous medical procedure that caused a

life-threatening reaction in several patients recently _____

_____

_____

_____

_____

ANSWERS

Algorithms and Heuristics

1. The Lost Cat:
   a. Look in every possible place following a systematic plan. For example, start in one room and search it completely. Then close the door and go to the next room and search it.
   b. Look first in places where Freeway has been found previously.

2. Sisters and Brothers:
   b. Many people use the representativeness heuristic, thinking that a sequence of four girls followed by four boys (or four heads followed by four tails, in an analogous situation) is not representative of those kinds of sequences. Actually, each possibility is equally likely (do you know why each is equally likely?)

3. IQ Scores:

b. Knowing the base rate in this problem should result in you selecting the first group of scores as more likely.

Multiple Choice

1. a
2. d
3. b
4. d
5. a

6. b
7. c
8. c
9. c

Chapter 21 -- Beliefs Are Supported by Powerful Biases

(or Why We're Often Wrong Even When We're Sure We're Right)

Checking Your Knowledge:
Terms, Statements, & Questions

After you have read this chapter, you should be able to define the terms/concepts, explain the statements, and answer the questions in this section *in your own words*. When appropriate, it may help to give a concrete example of the term or statement. It is most helpful if you try to answer in your own words before looking in the textbook.

1. confirmation bias _____

_____

2. Confirmation bias thrives because people generally focus on positive information. _____

_____

_____

3. Confirmation bias thrives because people don't easily consider alternatives. _____

_____

_____

4. Confirmation bias thrives because people tend not to look for contrary facts. _____

_____

_____

5. Confirmation bias thrives because people tend to explain away contrary facts when they happen.

_____

_____

6. Do shooting streaks really occur more often that one would expect by chance? Summarize the

results of the Gilovich, Vallone, and Tversky study on the "hot hand" in basketball. _____

_____

_____

_____

_____

_____

_____

Expanding Your Knowledge and Understanding: Problem Solving

Imagine you are an archeologist working on a dig on a small island in the Pacific Ocean. One day you discover a very old clay pot. You know that many centuries ago, the people on the two neighboring islands, Salomay and Dalton, both made beautiful clay pots (about 100 total on each island). You want to know which island this particular pot probably came from. The pots are known for two specific features: their handles (either rounded or square) and their texture (either smooth or rough). The pot you found has rounded handles and a smooth texture. From your studies, you remember that about 70% of all the pots made on Salomay had rounded handles, but you can't remember anything else.

Now imagine that you have just enough money left on your phone card to make a one-minute call back home to your professor, so you can only ask him <u>one</u> of the following questions:

    (a) What percentage of pots from Salomay had a smooth texture?

    (b) What percentage of pots from Dalton had a smooth texture?

    (c) What percentage of pots from Dalton had rounded handles?

1. Which piece of information would be the most helpful to you (and thus, you would choose to ask your professor about)? Why? _____

_____

_____

_____

2. Does choosing any of these options suggest a type of confirmation bias? If so, which option(s), and what type of confirmation bias? _____

_____

Testing Your Knowledge and Understanding:
Multiple Choice Questions

1. When asked why confirmation bias thrives, four students offered the following reasons. Who gave an inappropriate answer?
   a. Dale: "Because people ignore contrary facts."
   b. Maria: "Because people explain away contrary facts."
   c. Mark: "Because people determine that alternatives are insufficient explanations."
   d. Eric: "Because people focus on positive information."

2. Doug's car was recently hit by a teenage driver -- the third such event in ten years. He argues that teenagers are the worst drivers in the world. He does not mention that none of his four children, ranging in age from 16 to 30, have had any accidents, and that he personally has caused 5 accidents in the last 5 years. His comments about teenage drivers is an example of
   a. the availability heuristic
   b. confirmation bias
   c. the representativeness heuristic
   d. insight

3. Travis learns that his soon-to-be neighbor loves beer and ice hockey but does not enjoy wine or opera. He concludes that his neighbor is more likely to be a contract builder than a physician. His conclusion is an example of
   a. the availability heuristic
   b. the representativeness heuristic
   c. confirmation bias
   d. framing effects

Applying Your Knowledge and Understanding:
Belief in Astrology and Horoscopes

Nancy is a strong believer in astrology and her horoscope. In fact, she will not get out of bed each morning until she reads her horoscope. The slightest warning that the day may "bring trouble" results in Nancy spending the day in bed. She plans her personal and business life around her horoscope.

How would Nancy respond to each of the following occurrences? How would you explain Nancy's behavior in each instance?

1. Most of what her horoscope predicted for one day occurred. _____

_____

_____

_____

_____

2. Only 1 of 7 predictions occurred. _____

_____

_____

_____

_____

3. After showing a friend a horoscope reading for a day when absolutely everything that was predicted occurred, her friend asked her how many other days such perfection in the horoscope predictions Nancy had.

_____

_____

_____

_____

_____

4. After confirming most of what was predicted in a horoscope that was read to her by a friend, Nancy is told that the friend intentionally read the wrong sign. In fact, Nancy's real horoscope reading for that day contradicted most of what Nancy said actually happened.

_____

_____

_____

_____

ANSWERS

Problem Solving

If you chose to ask (a) and found out that 60% of the pots from Salomay had a smooth texture, what would you conclude about the likely origin of the pot you found? If you chose to ask (b) and found out that 90% of the pots from Dalton had a smooth texture, what would you conclude about the likely origin of the pot you found? If you chose to ask (c) and found out that 95% of the pots from Dalton had rounded handles, what would you conclude about the likely origin of the pot you found?

The best option is to get information about the alternative hypothesis, in this case, option (c), so you can compare the "data" you already have (70% of the pots from Salomay had rounded handles) with the same sort of data regarding the alternative (95% of the pots from Dalton had rounded handles). You began by knowing something about the pots on Salomay, that 70% had rounded handles, so you probably thought it was pretty likely the pot you found was from Salomay. Getting more information about that same hypothesis (that it came from Salomay) -- that 60% had a smooth texture -- would serve to confirm your hypothesis. But what if you instead found out information about the alternative hypothesis (that it came from Dalton) -- that 95% of the pots from Dalton had rounded handles? That would tell you that it's more likely your pot came from Dalton.

Remember, confirmation bias (in this case, not paying attention to alternatives) will not *always* lead you to a poor judgment (after all, it's possible that the pot actually is from Salomay)...but avoiding confirmation bias, now that you understand it, is more likely to lead you to better judgments.

Multiple Choice

1. c
2. b
3. b

Chapter 22 -- Behavior Affects Beliefs

(or Why the Marines Send Their Recruits to Boot Camp)

Checking Your Knowledge:
Terms, Statements, & Questions

After you have read this chapter, you should be able to define the terms/concepts, explain the statements, and answer the questions in this section *in your own words*. When appropriate, it may help to give a concrete example of the term or statement. It is most helpful if you try to answer in your own words before looking in the textbook.

1. cognitive dissonance
   theory
   _____

   _____

2. foot-in-the-door
   technique
   _____

   _____

3. insufficient justification
   effect
   _____

   _____

4. justification of investment
   _____

   _____

5. Behavior affects beliefs. _____

_____

_____

6. The dissonance experienced when there is inconsistency between belief and behavior is aversive

   and causes an individual to seek consistency. _____

_____

_____

7. According to the justification of investment, the more people invest in something, the more they

   like it. _____

_____

8. The perception of choice in behavior is a necessary condition for the behavior to affect beliefs.

_____

_____

9. The perception of meaningful consequences of behavior is a necessary condition for behavior to affect beliefs. _____

_____

_____

10. How do the results of the Festinger and Carlsmith study (the peg-turning task) support cognitive dissonance theory? _____

_____

_____

_____

_____

11. Why are fraternity pledges and Marine recruits put through such difficult initiations? _____

_____

_____

_____

Expanding Your Knowledge and Understanding:
Cognitive Dissonance in Practice

Cara, an 18-year-old college freshman, had been dating two men for several months. She liked both of them very much. Her roommate was always encouraging her to pick one of the men and get serious. But Cara said that she just wasn't certain if she loved either of the men.

After Cara came back to school after the semester break, she told her roommate that she was "so in love." When her roommate asked what happened, Cara explained that "Matt came to visit during the break. He convinced me to have sex with him and afterwards I realized that I really do love him. And now I know he's the one for me!"

How could cognitive dissonance theory explain Cara's story?

_____

_____

_____

_____

_____

_____

Testing Your Knowledge and Understanding:
Multiple Choice Questions

1. Which question would a cognitive dissonance researcher be most likely to address?
   a. Why do people engage in behavior that is contrary to their past behavior?
   b. Why do people receive pleasure from engaging in dissonant behavior?
   c. What happens when people engage in behavior that is inconsistent with the behavior of their peers?
   d. What happens when people engage in behavior that is inconsistent with their own beliefs?

2. A strict vegetarian, Lynn has just eaten a juicy hamburger at a going-away party for a good friend. According to cognitive dissonance theory, Lynn
   a. will be able to cope with the inconsistent behavior.
   b. is experiencing uncomfortable feelings because of her discrepant behavior.
   c. will feel okay about her behavior because she can blame her peers at the party.
   d. will become even more adamant about her vegetarianism.

3. Which of these factors may negate the effect of cognitive dissonance?
   a. the consequence of the belief-inconsistent behavior is significant
   b. the individual does not believe that she has any choice
   c. the individual perceives that the belief-inconsistent behavior is a personal choice
   d. the belief with which the behavior is inconsistent is a core belief

4. The core idea of the theory of cognitive dissonance is that
   a. inconsistency between beliefs and behavior is unusual
   b. individuals feel uncomfortable when they engage in behavior that is inconsistent with their beliefs.
   c. beliefs that make us feel dissonance should undergo extinction
   d. only dissonance that persists for a period of time should be addressed

5. Cognitive dissonance should not be experienced unless
   a. the person's behavior was voluntary
   b. the person's behavior was coerced
   c. the person's behavior disturbs others in his life
   d. the belief is shared by others

6. Which of the following individuals is most likely experiencing cognitive dissonance?
   a. Joyce, who does not believe in physical punishment but was slapped by her husband
   b. Donna, who believes that marriage is forever and stays with her abusive husband
   c. Karen, a vegetarian who refuses to wear leather
   d. Tracy, who does not believe in physical punishment and spanked her son

7. Elizabeth realized that when she received her copy of an exam that the teaching assistant had apparently given her the scoring sheet for the exam. She had never cheated before and after thinking about it, she copied the answers onto her scantron, handed in her scantron, and left. Cognitive dissonance theory would predict that she would tell a friend
   a. she was a bad person for cheating
   b. it really was not cheating since she had really studied hard for the test and probably would have done well
   c. it is not cheating if the teaching assistant was careless enough to hand her the scored test
   d. she would tell her instructor about the mistake later in the semester

8. A door-to-door encyclopedia salesperson who is familiar with the foot-in-the-door technique is likely to
   a. offer parents a bonus if they buy a set of books
   b. talk up his company before showing the books
   c. ask parents to complete a questionnaire about what they could do to help their children's education
   d. offer a full refund if the parents changed their minds

9. How much cognitive dissonance a person feels is affected by
   a. the number of times it has been experienced previously
   b. the level of justification for the behavior-discrepant behavior
   c. the presence of others
   d. the type of behavior displayed

10. Anna and Arthur attended a seminar entitled "How to Make Millions Sitting at Home." Even though their friends indicated that they read that the seminar speaker has been arrested for fraud, Anna and Arthur are likely to talk about how good the seminar was if
    a. many people attended
    b. they paid several hundred dollars each to attend
    c. they had been given the tickets to the seminar by a close relative
    d. they had made friends at the seminar

11. Which of the following is an example of the foot-in-the-door technique?
    a. At a grocery store, shoppers who eat a free sample of muffins are then handed a package of muffins to buy
    b. At a grocery store, shoppers are offered a coupon for 50 cents off muffins if they buy two packages
    c. A student explains that her father is a professor, and she needed to turn in a term paper one day late
    d. A friend asked if he could borrow $200 and, after you said no, asked if you would loan him $20

Applying Your Knowledge and Understanding: Challenge

You have been hired by a small town to help them address some social problems they are experiencing. Prejudice and discrimination toward various groups have placed their community in jeopardy and they are seeking ways to reduce these problems. How could cognitive dissonance theory be employed in addressing the various "-isms," such as racism and sexism, that the community is experiencing? What specific recommendations would you make?

_____

_____

_____

_____

_____

_____

_____

In light of your plans, what issues might be raised by confirmation biases discussed earlier? How would you deal with these issues?

_____

_____

_____

_____

_____

_____

ANSWERS

Multiple Choice

1. d	7. c
2. b	8. c
3. b	9. b
4. b	10. b
5. a	11. a
6. d	

Chapter 23 -- People Are Not Always Consciously Aware of the Causes of Their Behavior

(or Why Freud Was Right--about Some Things)

Checking Your Knowledge:
Terms, Statements, & Questions

After you have read this chapter, you should be able to define the terms/concepts, explain the statements, and answer the questions in this section *in your own words*. When appropriate, it may help to give a concrete example of the term or statement. It is most helpful if you try to answer in your own words before looking in the textbook.

1. absolute threshold

2. ego

3. id

4. psychoanalytic theory

5. subliminal mere exposure effect

6. superego

7. The ego is fundamentally guided by the reality principle.

8. The core of Freud's theory is that the causes of many of our thoughts, feelings, and behaviors lie outside of conscious awareness. _____

_____

_____

9. The bystander intervention effect illustrates the idea that people are sometimes unaware of the situational causes of their behavior. _____

_____

_____

10. Describe Freud's three states of consciousness. _____

_____

_____

_____

11. In Freud's theory, how are neurotic anxiety, moral anxiety, and repression related? _____

_____

_____

_____

12. What are criticisms of Freud's theory? _____

_____

_____

13. What do the authors conclude about whether subliminal perception exists? _____

_____

_____

14. What is mindlessness? _____

_____

15. How did Langer's studies on allowing people to cut in line to use a photocopier and returning a university memo demonstrate mindlessness? _____

_____

_____

_____

16. How did the split-brain patient known as "P.S." respond when an emotionally tinged word was presented only to his *right* hemisphere? _____

_____

_____

17. How is the research done with P.S. evidence for the idea that people are not always consciously aware of the causes of their behavior? _____

_____

_____

_____

18. What did you learn in Part 6 (chapters 20, 21, 22, and 23) that supports the Basic Idea that "humans have the ability to think and reason in *very* powerful ways, but we also have a number of cognitive limitations that lead to systematic errors?" _____

_____

_____

_____

19. What did you learn in Part 6 that supports the Basic Idea that "you cannot understand psychology without understanding evolution. Behavior results from an interaction between genetic factors and the immediate situation?" _____

_____

_____

_____

_____

20. What did you learn in Part 6 that supports the Basic Idea that "many cognitive limitations can be overcome by using cognitive tools?" _____

_____

_____

_____

21. What did you learn in Part 6 that supports the Basic Idea that "adaptation is *the* fundamental property of human behavior and cognition?" _____

_____

_____

_____

_____

Expanding Your Knowledge and Understanding:
Unconscious Behavior

1. Besides flushing the toilet, what other "mindless" behaviors do you exhibit on a regular basis? What mindless behaviors have you seen other people do? What role might schemas and scripts play in these behaviors?

_____

_____

_____

_____

_____

_____

2. One of the reasons the authors discussed Freud's theories in this chapter is that Freud is a prominent name associated with psychology in our culture. You have probably heard of a "Freudian slip," usually a verbal type of mistake. For example, as you and a friend are heading out of your dorm room to go to the library and study, you tell your roommate, "We're off to the bar" instead. Freud believed these slips were not so much mistakes as they were unconscious conflicts trying to get out...in this case, he would probably say that your id wanted the pleasure of going to the bar instead of the pain of going to the library. Cognitive psychologists, on the other hand, generally favor a more cognitive explanation for such mistakes, that they are likely just by-products of how our minds process information and direct behavior. For example, the most common type of slip seems to be one in which a strong habit or frequent activity/behavior is the intrusion.

Have you ever been accused of a Freudian slip? What was it? Which do you think is a better explanation for Freudian slips? How might this cognitive explanation be related to "mindlessness?"

Testing Your Knowledge and Understanding:
Multiple Choice Questions

1. When one-month old Sonya starts crying at 3 a.m., her parents know she's probably just hungry. Freud would say her crying is driven by the
   a. ego
   b. id
   c. superego
   d. perceptual-conscious

2. Jason comes home from school hungry and wants a snack. Just as he's about to sneak some cookies from the forbidden cookie jar, he hears his mom coming in the back door. He quickly closes the cookie jar without any cookies and heads to his room to do homework. Freud would say Jason's _____ drove him to close the cookie jar.
   a. ego
   b. id
   c. superego
   d. perceptual-conscious

3. Lauren is visiting at her friend's house for the evening. After dinner, when her friend left the room to feed her dog, Lauren notices her friend's mother left her purse on the counter when she went out for a walk. Lauren knows she could take money from her friend's mother's wallet, but she doesn't do it. According to Freud's theory, Lauren's decision was driven by her
   a. ego
   b. id
   c. superego
   d. perceptual-conscious

Applying Your Knowledge and Understanding: Challenge

Not long ago, repressed memories were a popular topic among talk shows and courtroom dramas. Repressed memories were generally a person's memories of being abused (usually sexually) as a young child that were thought to be completely repressed into that person's unconscious because they were too painful to deal with. Thus, the person goes through life not even realizing he or she was abused until something triggers the memory later in life, and it comes into consciousness.

1. If you were a lawyer defending someone accused of sexual abuse on the basis of a repressed memory, what would you do?

_____

_____

_____

_____

_____

2. If you were a lawyer prosecuting a case based on a repressed memory, what would you do?

_____

_____

_____

_____

3. Obviously a controlled experiment is impossible to conduct, but is there any other way you could gather data relevant to the question of whether repressed memories are reflective of events that actually happened?

_____

_____

_____

_____

_____

ANSWERS

Multiple Choice

1. b
2. a
3. c

Chapter 24 -- Early Experience Has a Major Impact on Later Behavior

(or Why Brothers and Sisters Rarely Marry Each Other)

Checking Your Knowledge:
Terms, Statements, & Questions

After you have read this chapter, you should be able to define the terms/concepts, explain the statements, and answer the questions in this section *in your own words*. When appropriate, it may help to give a concrete example of the term or statement. It is most helpful if you try to answer in your own words before looking in the textbook.

1. critical period _____

_____

2. imprinting _____

_____

3. Westermark hypothesis _____

_____

4. Although bioprogramming works most of the time, it can be sensitive to environmental changes.

_____

_____

_____

5. Early experience influences brain structure and brain chemistry in some species. _____

_____

_____

6. Deprivation of sensory stimulation and social contact has profound developmental effects in

humans. _____

_____

_____

7. Early experience appears to affect adult sexual behavior. _____

_____

_____

8. What evidence is given in the text for the hypothesis that early experience has a major impact on

human development? _____

_____

_____

_____

9. How can the incest taboo be explained by evolutionary theory? _____

_____

_____

_____

10. How is it explained using the concept of negative imprinting? _____

_____

_____

_____

Expanding Your Knowledge and Understanding:
Critical Periods for Bonding in Humans?

Some psychologists have presented a controversial proposal regarding bonding in humans. It has been proposed that there is a critical period for mother-infant bonding. Specifically, the first hour after an infant's birth has been identified as the critical time for this bonding to occur. One critical factor that has been hypothesized to promote bonding is the extensive skin-to-skin contact shared by a newborn and his/her mother immediately after birth (Klaus, Kennell, & Klaus, 1995). (It should be noted that this proposed critical period has not been empirically supported to date.)

1. How could this hypothesized critical period be investigated scientifically? What research issues would be confronted in such research?

_____

_____

_____

_____

_____

2. What are the implications of this proposed critical period for the child?

_____

_____

_____

_____

_____

3. What are the implications of this proposed critical period for mothers?

_____

_____

_____

_____

_____

4. What are the implications of this proposed critical period for fathers?

_____

_____

_____

5. What are the implications of this proposed critical period for adoptive parents?

_____

_____

_____

_____

_____

6. Why do you suppose this critical period is controversial?

_____

_____

_____

_____

_____

Testing Your Knowledge and Understanding: Multiple Choice Questions

1. An innate learning involving attachment to the first moving object seen is
   a. instinct
   b. imprinting
   c. modeling
   d. bonding

2. Which student offered the best description of the relationship between biology and the environment in terms of development?
    a. Chris: "Environment is more important."
    b. Artie: "Biology is more important."
    c. Mike: "Environment and biology interact."
    d. Ken: "Environment and biology are independent of each other."

3. Which seems to be the most likely factor underlying the incest taboo?
    a. positive imprinting
    b. social learning
    c. biological imperatives
    d. negative imprinting

4. The impact of the social isolation on monkeys
    a. was short lived
    b. lasted at least one year
    c. had a long-term impact on females but not males
    d. continued for more than three years

5. The primary characteristic of critical periods in development is
    a. significant and temporary behavioral changes
    b. rapid and relatively permanent learning
    c. major conflict
    d. strong emotional reactions

6. Given the results of the Harlows' research with monkeys, first-time parents of newborn infants should be reminded that
    a. newborns have critical physical needs at birth but emotional needs are slower to appear
    b. newborns have minimal emotional needs but that the parents should address these needs when possible
    c. the emotional needs of newborns are every bit as important as physical needs
    d. by meeting the physical needs, the newborn's emotional needs will be met

7. Which student offered a true statement about the impact of sensory stimulation and social contact deprivation on children?
    a. Burton: "Such deprivation affects intellectual/emotional development but not the appearance of physical milestones like sitting up and rolling over."
    b. Boyd: "Such deprivation delays the appearance of physical milestones like sitting up and rolling over but not intellectual/emotional development."
    c. Mel: "Such early deprivation has serious consequences for the child's development but the consequences disappear at about age six."
    d. Hallie: "We don't really know if the consequences of such deprivation are temporary or permanent - only that the longer the deprivation lasts, the more serious the long-term consequences."

Applying Your Knowledge and Understanding: Challenge

An appreciation of the importance of early experience on subsequent development has received increased attention over the last decade. Recently, one "child expert" told expectant parents to "teach" their fetuses -- reading to the fetus, playing music through earphones placed on the mother's stomach, and speaking a foreign language to the fetus.

1. Do such recommendations seem reasonable in light of the information in this chapter?

_____

_____

_____

_____

2. How could you test the hypothesis that "playing music through earphones placed on the expectant mother's abdomen has positive effects on an infant's subsequent development?" What effects do you think might be seen?

_____

_____

_____

_____

3. What recommendations would you put forth for new parents to foster their child's development? Be as specific as you can.

_____

_____

_____

_____

ANSWERS

Multiple Choice

1. b
2. c
3. d
4. d
5. b
6. c
7. d

REFERENCE

Klaus, P. H., Kennel, J. H., & Klaus, M. H. (1995). *Bonding: Building the foundations of secure attachment and independence.* Reading, MA: Addison-Wesley.

Chapter 25 -- A Child Is Not a Miniature Adult

(or Why You Should Expect Your Child to Act Like a Child)

Checking Your Knowledge:
Terms, Statements, & Questions

After you have read this chapter, you should be able to define the terms/concepts, explain the statements, and answer the questions in this section *in your own words*. When appropriate, it may help to give a concrete example of the term or statement. It is most helpful if you try to answer in your own words before looking in the textbook.

1. accommodation _____

   _____

2. assimilation _____

   _____

3. conservation _____

   _____

4. egocentrism _____

   _____

5. object permanence _____

   _____

6. According to Piaget, children pass through an orderly, predictable sequence of stages of thought that requires that the child master particular fundamental cognitive skills before developing

   others. _____

   _____

   _____

7. Piaget proposed that the development of a set of conceptual structures results from the interaction of biology and the environment. _____

8. Two processes involved in the biology--environment interaction are (a) accommodation _____

_____

_____

and (b) assimilation _____

_____

9. The child's interactions with the environment result in the development of schemas. _____

_____

_____

_____

10. Children are cognitively egocentric. _____

_____

_____

_____

11. Children and adults do not understand physical causality in the same way. _____

_____

_____

_____

12. Children and adults do not understand social causality in the same way. _____

_____

_____

_____

13. Children and adults do not understand classification in the same way. _____

_____

_____

_____

_____

14. Children and adults do not understand "at the same time" in the same way. _____

_____

_____

_____

15. Children and adults do not understand age in the same way. _____

_____

_____

_____

16. How are Piaget's stages universal, sequential, and qualitative? _____

_____

_____

_____

_____

17. In your own words, describe Piaget's four stages of cognitive development, noting the

approximate ages at which each begins and the characteristics of each stage:

(a) sensorimotor _____

_____

_____

(b) preoperational _____

_____

_____

(c) concrete operations _____

_____

_____

(d) formal operations _____

_____

_____

Expanding Your Knowledge and Understanding:
Accommodation and Assimilation

1. One day, three-year-old Kayla went to the grocery store with her mother, her grandmother, and her aunt. As they were checking out, Kayla, sitting in the shopping cart, cried, "Mom." Immediately Kayla's mother responded -- only to be rejected by Kayla, who said, "No, not you -- Mom!" Her grandmother (who was called "Mom" by everyone in the family) then answered, asking what Kayla wanted. Somewhat frustrated, Kayla cried, "Not you...Aunt Mom."

Discuss this episode in terms of Piaget's concepts of

(a) schema _____

_____

_____

_____

(b) assimilation _____

_____

_____

_____

and (c) accommodation _____

_____

_____

_____

2. When was the last time you engaged in accommodation and/or assimilation? _____

_____

_____

_____

Testing Your Knowledge and Understanding: Multiple Choice Questions

1. When they have beets for dinner, Susie asks her father to cut hers in half because then "I have twice as much to eat." It is obvious that Susie has not yet mastered
   a. object permanence
   b. conservation
   c. syncretism
   d. physical causality

2. Which of the following is not an example of Piaget's concept of egocentrism?
   a. Little Luke brings his crying mother the teddy bear he hugs when he's scared.
   b. For his birthday, Clara buys her father her very favorite movie -- "Bambi."
   c. Ashley covers her eyes and says to her brother, "Now you can't see me."
   d. Julie brings her father his slippers on Father's Day.

3. Eight month old Suzette loves to play with a stuffed dog her uncle gave her. However, when her mother takes the dog away, Suzette watches her put it in the toy chest. Then Suzette begins playing with another toy, acting as if the dog never existed. Suzette's behavior demonstrates a lack of
   a. physical causality
   b. conservation
   c. object permanence
   d. syncretism

4. Christie thinks all boys are horrible and refuses to play with any boy. However, when Ian moved in next door, Christie thought he was pretty nice and invited him to her "school's out" party. He was the only boy she invited. Christie's response to Ian necessitated
   a. a change in her social causality
   b. assimilation
   c. accommodation
   d. a change in her social simultaneity

5. Babies can play peek-a-boo for hours because
   a. they have not yet developed egocentrism
   b. they have not yet developed conservation
   c. they have not yet developed object permanence
   d. they have not yet developed causality

6. A child who bullies his younger sister to get what he wants also bullies the other children in the neighborhood. This child's behavior reflects
   a. accommodation
   b. assimilation
   c. conservation
   d. object permanence

7. When asked why it gets dark at night, Carmen says "The sun goes to bed so I can go to bed and sleep in the dark." Carmen's response reflects
   a. accommodation
   b. assimilation
   c. syncretism
   d. factual confusion

8. Which of Piaget's stages is characterized, in part, by the ability to take the perspective of other people, and the understanding of conservation?
   a. concrete operations
   b. formal operations
   c. sensorimotor
   d. preoperational

9. Which of Piaget's stages is characterized, in part, by interaction with the world through grasping, feeling, sucking, and tasting, and the accomplishment of object permanence?
   a. concrete operations
   b. formal operations
   c. sensorimotor
   d. preoperational

10. Which of Piaget's stages is characterized, in part, by the ability to think abstractly and to test hypotheses systematically?
    a. concrete operations
    b. formal operations
    c. sensorimotor
    d. preoperational

11. Which if Piaget's stages is characterized, in part, by continued egocentrism and the ability to represent the world in pictures and words?
    a. concrete operations
    b. formal operations
    c. sensorimotor
    d. preoperational

Applying Your Knowledge and Understanding: Challenge

In light of Piaget's stage theory of cognitive development and the awareness that children do not think like adults, adults must modify their behavior when interacting with children. This is an issue particularly for teachers of young children.

1. What stage are nursery school students (about ages 3-5) likely to be in? What characterizes cognition at this stage? How does that suggest adjustments that a nursery school teacher must make to be effective with his or her students?

_____

_____

_____

_____

_____

2. What stage are third graders (about age 8 or 9) likely to be in? What characterizes cognition at this stage? How does that suggest adjustments that a third grade teacher must make to be effective with his or her students?

_____

_____

ANSWERS

Accommodation and Assimilation

1. (a) Kayla's schema of mothers is all adult women.
   (b) Kayla uses "Mom" to call all adult women in her family. It works for her mother and everyone in the family calls her grandmother "Mom." So it is reasonable to her that her aunt also answers to "Mom."
   (c) When her aunt does not answer when Kayla calls her "Mom," she has to alter her thinking and calls her "Aunt Mom."

2. Since we don't stop learning in adulthood, we assimilate and accommodate everyday (although in ways that are very different from the assimilation and accommodation that children do).

Multiple Choice

1. b	7. c
2. d	8. a
3. c	9. c
4. c	10. b
5. c	11. d
6. b	

Chapter 26 -- Humans Have a Biologically Programmed Capacity for Language

(or Why Children, but Not Chimpanzees, Easily Master English)

Checking Your Knowledge:
Terms, Statements, & Questions

After you have read this chapter, you should be able to define the terms/concepts, explain the statements, and answer the questions in this section *in your own words*. When appropriate, it may help to give a concrete example of the term or statement. It is most helpful if you try to answer in your own words before looking in the textbook.

1. generative grammar _____

_____

2. morpheme _____

_____

3. phoneme _____

_____

4. Language uses a small set of arbitrary symbols. _____

_____

5. The combination of arbitrary symbols into morphemes and words is rule-bound. _____

_____

_____

6. Words are combined into sentences via a set of rules. _____

_____

_____

7. High school English teachers are concerned with prescriptive rules whereas linguists and

psycholinguists focus on descriptive rules. _____

_____

8. All languages appear to share a universal grammar. _____

_____

_____

9. Humans appear to have a biological predisposition for language acquisition. _____

_____

_____

10. Regardless of the language being learned, there is a regular, predictable sequence in the

learning process. _____

_____

_____

11. The operant model does not account sufficiently for language acquisition. _____

_____

_____

12. There appears to be a critical period for language acquisition in humans. _____

_____

_____

13. Non-human animals communicate, but not using a language. _____

_____

_____

14. How does Noam Chomsky's idea of a universal grammar support the hypothesis that language

has a biological/evolutionary component? _____

_____

_____

15. How does the way children learn language support the hypothesis that language has a

   biological/evolutionary component? _____

   _____

   _____

16. What did you learn in Part 7 (chapters 24, 25, and 26) that supports the Basic Idea that *"much*

   human behavior results from an interaction between past experience and the immediate

   situation?" _____

   _____

   _____

   _____

17. What did you learn in Part 7 that supports the Basic Idea that "you cannot understand

   psychology without understanding evolution. Behavior results from an interaction between

   genetic factors and the immediate situation?" _____

   _____

   _____

   _____

Expanding Your Knowledge and Understanding: Theories of Language Acquisition

1. Compare the two theories of language acquisition by filling in the table below.

Theorist	Primary Factor Underlying Acquisition	What Child Learns	Processes or Mechanisms of Learning
Chomsky			
Skinner/ behaviorists			

2. When young Austin returned from the store, he told his father: "I goed to the store and Mommy buyed shoes for my feets."

   (a) How would Chomsky explain Austin's statement? _____

   _____

   _____

   _____

   _____

   _____

(b) How would Skinner explain Austin's statement? _____

_____

_____

_____

_____

_____

(c) Which do you think is a better explanation for language acquisition? _____

_____

_____

_____

_____

_____

Testing Your Knowledge and Understanding: Multiple Choice Questions

1. A general principle about language development is that
   a. parental instruction is a necessary component
   b. there is a universal sequence
   c. morphemes precede phoneme learning
   d. morphemes and phonemes are meaningless until syntax is learned

2. Which concept is inconsistent with the others?
   a. imitation
   b. behaviorism
   c. biological predisposition
   d. reinforcement

3. _____ controls how language is learned and _____ determines what language a child learns.
   a. Environment; biology
   b. Biology; environment
   c. Reinforcement; modeling
   d. Modeling; reinforcement

4. The sentence "Brother school went my" violates
   a. phoneme rules
   b. syntax
   c. morpheme rules
   d. linguistic criteria

5. The smallest unit of speech that carries a meaning is
   a. a word
   b. a morpheme
   c. syntax
   d. a phoneme

6. The sounds "ch," "b," "l," and "th" are
   a. morphemes
   b. semantics
   c. phonemes
   d. syntax

7. In English, there are
   a. an equal number of phonemes and morphemes
   b. more phonemes than morphemes
   c. more morphemes than phonemes
   d. a known number of morphemes and an unlimited number of phonemes

8. Babbling behavior begins at about age
   a. 1 month
   b. 3 months
   c. 6 months
   d. 8 months

9. Children learn a language in the following order
   a. phoneme -> morpheme -> words
   b. morpheme -> phoneme -> words
   c. phoneme -> words -> morpheme
   d. morpheme -> words -> phoneme

10. Which student shows the best understanding of efforts to teach language to nonhuman animals?
    a. Kerri: "Chimpanzees have shown considerable success in learning language."
    b. Nash: "Chimpanzees have language abilities equivalent to a lot of 6-year-olds."
    c. Willard: "Chimpanzees can learn thousands of words."
    d. Mark: "Chimpanzees can learn some words but their word combinations are almost random."

11. For all children, regardless of the language learned, language begins with
    a. morphemes
    b. phonemes
    c. babbling
    d. syntax

Applying Your Knowledge and Understanding: Challenge

At the end of this chapter, the authors state that language acquisition is a powerful example of both the biological influences on behavior and the idea that behavior that is adaptive in an evolutionary sense is selected for. What arguments can you make to support this claim?

_____

_____

_____

_____

_____

_____

_____

_____

_____

ANSWERS

Theories of Language Acquisition

1.

Theorist		Primary Factor Underlying Acquisition	What Child Learns	Processes or Mechanisms of Learning
	Chomsky	biological determinism	rules of language	language acquisition device
	Skinner/behaviorists	environment	specific verbalization	imitation and reinforcement

2. Chomsky: Children learn rules of language. Austin's statement reflects that he has learned the basic rule of adding "-ed" for past tense and "s" for plural. He has not learned the exceptions yet.

   Skinner: Since Skinner argues that imitation and reinforcement are the processes for language acquisition, he would have a more difficult time explaining Austin's statement -- unless, of course, he has an older sibling or adults in his world who talk like this.

Multiple Choice

1. b	7. c
2. c	8. c
3. b	9. a
4. b	10. d
5. b	11. c
6. c	

Chapter 27 -- Social Influence Is One of the Most Powerful Determinants of Human Behavior

(or Why Someone Who Grows Up in Iraq Is More Likely to be a Muslim Than a Christian)

Checking Your Knowledge: Terms, Statements, & Questions

After you have read this chapter, you should be able to define the terms/concepts, explain the statements, and answer the questions in this section *in your own words*. When appropriate, it may help to give a concrete example of the term or statement. It is most helpful if you try to answer in your own words before looking in the textbook.

1. attribution theory _____

   _____

2. external attributions _____

   _____

3. fundamental attribution error _____

   _____

4. group norm _____

   _____

5. internal attributions _____

   _____

6. social influence _____

   _____

7. Human social behavior is homogeneous within groups and heterogeneous between groups.

   _____

   _____

8. The number of people present affects degree of social influence. _____

   _____

9. Even one other nonconforming person decreases the level of conformity to group pressure.

_____

_____

10. How do Sherif's and Asch's studies provide evidence for the argument that people's behavior is strongly influenced by their social environment? _____

_____

_____

_____

11. Why was there such a discrepancy between what people *predicted* they and others would do and what the subjects actually *did* in Milgram's obedience study? _____

_____

_____

_____

_____

Expanding Your Knowledge and Understanding: Conditions of Social Influence

1. The United States is identified as an individualist society in that we emphasize personal goals over group goals. In contrast, China is a collectivist society that puts group goals ahead of personal goals. We know that attributions may differ in individualist versus collectivist societies. Would citizens in these two types of societies differ in terms of response to social conformity? If so, how?

_____

_____

_____

_____

2. Do you think the rate of conformity would increase or decrease

    (a) with the use of an ambiguous task?   _____

    (b) when someone has self-doubt?   _____

    (c) when the judgments are recorded privately?   _____

    (d) when there is a high-status confederate?   _____

3. Explain Milgram's results in terms of the foot-in-the-door technique.

_____

_____

_____

_____

_____

4. In Williams v. Florida (1970), the Supreme Court declared that juries with as few as 6 jurors were constitutional. Through this decree, the Court declared that jury size should not affect jury verdicts.

    (a) If you were on trial for a serious crime, which would you rather have -- a 6-person jury or a 12-person jury? Explain your answer.

_____

_____

_____

_____

_____

    (b) Since Asch found that increasing group size after 5 does not greatly affect group pressure to conform, should a 6-person versus a 12-person jury make a difference?

_____

_____

_____

_____

_____

(c) Would you expect less conformity in a 6-person or a 12-person jury?

_____

_____

_____

_____

_____

_____

Testing Your Knowledge and Understanding:
Multiple Choice Questions

1. Conformity is
   a. the desire to be like others
   b. changing one's behavior in the direction of group norms
   c. changing beliefs but not behavior
   d. giving in to verbal commands

2. One way to prevent conformity in an Asch-like study, at least in an experimental setting, is
   a. to have an individual model nonconformity
   b. to use well-educated subjects
   c. to have at least one conservative subject
   d. to use young subjects

3. In which of the following conditions would you expect a research participant in a Milgram-type study not to obey the experimenter and stop delivering shocks to the "learner?"
   a. if the participant met the learner first
   b. if the participant learned that even one other participant refused to obey
   c. if the learner begged the participant to stop
   d. if the participant threatened the participant if he/she did not stop

4. People are _____ likely to obey authority in the real world than in the laboratory because _____.
   a. less; other influences are present
   b. less; they would have the opportunity to see the unreasonableness of the order
   c. more; in the real world authority figures have greater power
   d. more; they would not be held responsible

5. What student offered the best summary of the fundamental lesson from Milgram's obedience studies?
   a. Clay: "A basic level of aggression must be present for an authority figure to get someone to hurt another person."
   b. Pam: "Even nonhostile people can hurt others when told to do so by an authority figure."
   c. Lewis: "Only people with psychological hang-ups about hostility would be aggressive upon demand."
   d. Rob: "A good authority figure can bring repressed hostility to the surface."

6. When we make a fundamental attribution error, we place _____ emphasis on dispositional factors when explaining the behavior of others.
   a. just the right level of
   b. too much
   c. too little
   d. an unknown level of

7. When David was cut from the high school basketball team, his father believed that his son was cut because he was clumsy and not athletic. His mother argued that the coach didn't give her son the attention he needed to develop his skills. The father was demonstrating a(n) _____ while the mother was demonstrating a(n) _____.
   a. internal attribution; external attribution
   b. external attribution; internal attribution
   c. situational attribution; dispositional attribution
   d. dispositional attribution; internal attribution

Applying Your Knowledge and Understanding: Challenges

1. How can the results of social influence research be applied to address

   (a) improving conservation of water in men's dorms? _____

   _____

   _____

   _____

_____

_____

(b) increasing recycling on a college campus? _____

_____

_____

_____

_____

_____

2. What is the role of attributions and the fundamental attribution error in

(a) racial prejudice? _____

_____

_____

_____

_____

_____

(b) heterosexism or homophobia? _____

_____

_____

_____

_____

_____

and (c) sexism? _____

_____

ANSWERS

Conditions of Social Influence

1. There is generally greater conformity in collectivist societies where there is more importance placed on respect, group norms, and cooperation.

2. a. increase
   b. increase
   c. decrease
   d. increase

3. The participants initially obeyed small orders, so when the demand that higher shocks be delivered, the previous obedience increases the likelihood of obeying the subsequent, larger demands.

4. There is likely to be more pressure to conform in a 6-person jury than in a 12-person jury. In fact, a 12-person jury may exert less pressure to conform. It is more likely that a 6-person jury will have only one person voting against the majority -- a 1 in 6 chance. However, with a 12-person jury, it is more likely that at least 2 people will vote against the majority. Since having even one ally is critical according to Asch's research, a 12-person jury should be preferred.

Multiple Choice

1. b
2. a
3. b
4. c
5. b
6. b
7. a

Chapter 28 -- The Mere Presence of Other People Has a Substantial Effect on Behavior

(or Why Most Six-Year-Old Violinists Play More Poorly at a Recital Than at a Rehearsal)

Checking Your Knowledge:
Terms, Statements, & Questions

After you have read this chapter, you should be able to define the terms/concepts, explain the statements, and answer the questions in this section *in your own words*. When appropriate, it may help to give a concrete example of the term or statement. It is most helpful if you try to answer in your own words before looking in the textbook.

1. dominant response _____

_____

2. paradigm _____

_____

_____

3. response hierarchy _____

_____

4. social facilitation _____

_____

5. Scientists often see the world in paradigm-bound ways. _____

_____

_____

6. Paradigms are not easily abandoned. _____

_____

_____

7. In a performance situation, the presence of others facilitates performance because arousal increases the probability of doing the "right" thing. _____

_____

_____

8. In a learning situation, the presence of others leads to poorer learning because arousal increases the probability of doing the wrong thing. _____

_____

_____

9. Summarize the development of what we know about social facilitation. (a) What were the results of early studies? _____

_____

_____

_____

(b) How did Zajonc explain these conflicting results? _____

_____

_____

_____

(c) Why was his model then considered the paradigm for studying social facilitation? _____

_____

_____

_____

Expanding Your Knowledge and Understanding:
Paradigmatic Problems?

Paradigmatic research may be reflective of a real science. However, such research is not without its problems and negative consequences. What are some of them?

_____

_____

_____

_____

_____

_____

Expanding Your Knowledge and Understanding:
Racing the Clock

Sometimes in the Winter Olympics, speed skaters race with a competitor and sometimes alone. Since each skater is actually "racing against the clock," should it make any difference if someone skates alone or with others? Why or why not?

_____

_____

_____

_____

_____

_____

Testing Your Knowledge and Understanding:
Multiple Choice Questions

1. When Karen watches *Jeopardy!* at home, she knows the answers to about 80% of the questions. Her friends encouraged her to apply to be a contestant on the show. However, when she was a contestant and the show was videotaped before an audience, she found it difficult to give the right answer to even the easier questions. The discrepancy between her performance at home versus during the videotaping is probably the result of
   a. conformity
   b. social facilitation
   c. polarization
   d. performance anxiety

2. Which student displays the best understanding of social facilitation?
   a. Lionel: "When first learning a task, it is advantageous to practice around your closest friends because they provide uncritical support."
   b. Tara: "An individual always does better when alone than in front of an audience."
   c. Charlotte: "Dispositional factors must be considered - some people are extroverts and always want an audience and others are introverts who may sometimes perform better when alone."
   d. Judy: "If you are learning a difficult task, you will do better alone."

3. Marathon runners increase their speed on a race course that is lined by spectators. This is an example of
   a. social assistance
   b. social facilitation
   c. second wind
   d. "hitting the wall."

4. Which of the following tasks is not likely to be helped if observers are present?
   a. mowing the lawn
   b. solving a logic problem
   c. counting by 2's
   d. alphabetizing cards

5. Chet has a local televised cooking show on cable. He has noticed that the _____ of others _____ him when he is preparing easy recipes and the _____ of others _____ him when he is preparing hard recipes.
   a. presence; does not bother; presence; bothers
   b. absence; bothers; absence; bothers
   c. presence; bothers; presence; does not bother
   d. absence; does not bother; absence; bothers

Applying Your Knowledge and Understanding: Challenge

Consider how schools generally teach such skills as reading, spelling, computer use, and mathematics. After reading this chapter, what recommendations would you offer about the best way to teach such skills?

_____

_____

_____

_____

_____

_____

ANSWERS

Racing the Clock

Since the speed skating is so well-rehearsed, you would expect that a racer going against a competitor would have an edge over the skater racing only the clock.

Multiple Choice

1. b
2. d
3. b
4. b
5. a

Chapter 29 -- Cooperation Can Happen Even When Everyone Is Looking Out for Themselves

(or Why Some Soldiers in the Trenches in WWI Stopped Shooting at Each Other)

Checking Your Knowledge: Terms, Statements, & Questions

After you have read this chapter, you should be able to define the terms/concepts, explain the statements, and answer the questions in this section *in your own words*. When appropriate, it may help to give a concrete example of the term or statement. It is most helpful if you try to answer in your own words before looking in the textbook.

1. normative model _____

_____

2. prisoner's dilemma game _____

_____

3. tit for tat _____

_____

4. tragedy of the commons _____

_____

5. zero-sum game _____

_____

6. Many human interactions can be analyzed via game theory. _____

_____

_____

7. Mutual cooperation leads to high payoff at a relatively low cost. _____

_____

_____

8. What happens when both players in a prisoner's dilemma choose to compete? _____

_____

_____

9. What happens when both players in a prisoner's dilemma choose to cooperate? _____

_____

_____

10. Why would a tendency towards cooperation be adaptive, when conditions warrant it? _____

_____

_____

_____

11. What did you learn in Part 8 (chapters 27, 28, and 29) that supports the Basic Idea that "*much human behavior is influenced by other people?*" _____

_____

_____

_____

12. What did you learn in Part 8 that supports the Basic Idea that "you cannot understand psychology without understanding evolution. Behavior results from an interaction between genetic factors and the immediate situation?" _____

_____

_____

_____

13. What did you learn in Part 8 that supports the Basic Idea that "science is *by far* the most powerful way the human race has yet devised for understanding the world, including, of course, our own behavior?" _____

_____

_____

_____

Expanding Your Knowledge and Understanding: Panic Situations

All of us have heard the phrase "never yell fire in a crowded theater." Yet, large groups of people in locations with restricted exits generally panic in fires and other disasters. Roger Brown (1965) has suggested that the prisoner's dilemma can be applied to such situations. Create a payoff table (just like the ones in the text) for such an application of the prisoner's dilemma. This table should consider the behaviors of leaving a theater calmly or in a rush and the behavior of yourself and all others.

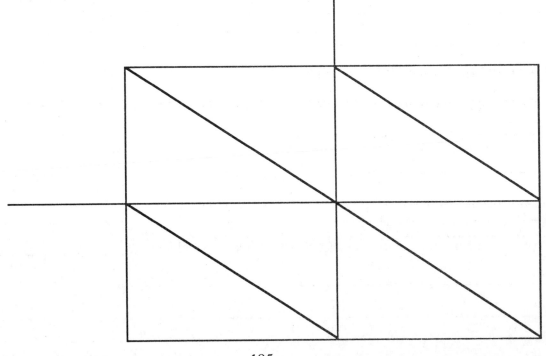

Using this table, explain why people panic in such situations.

_____

_____

_____

_____

_____

Applying Your Knowledge and Understanding: Challenges

1. How can you use the ideas in this chapter to explain the disappearance of the tropical rain forest?

_____

_____

_____

_____

2. Explain what role each of the following factors has in selecting a competitive or cooperative strategy in a prisoner's dilemma situation.

(a) ability to recognize different people _____

_____

_____

(b) remembering previous interactions with different people _____

_____

_____

and (c) communicating one's values _____

_____

_____

3. What is the relationship between trust and the selection of a strategy for the prisoner's dilemma?

_____

_____

_____

_____

REFERENCE

Brown, R. (1965). *Social psychology*. New York: Free Press, Macmillan.

Chapter 30 -- It Is Difficult, but Not Impossible, to Develop Meaningful Psychological Tests

(or Why You Can't Say You're Twice as Smart as Somebody Else)

Checking Your Knowledge: Terms, Statements, & Questions

After you have read this chapter, you should be able to define the terms/concepts, explain the statements, and answer the questions in this section *in your own words*. When appropriate, it may help to give a concrete example of the term or statement. It is most helpful if you try to answer in your own words before looking in the textbook.

1. arbitrary zero point

2. Barnum effect

3. construct

4. construct validity

5. face validity

6. individual differences

7. internal consistency

8. normal distribution

9. objectivity _____

_____

10. predictive validity _____

_____

11. reliability _____

_____

12. test-retest reliability _____

_____

13. true zero point _____

_____

14. validity _____

_____

15. validity criteria _____

_____

16. The field of psychological testing studies individual differences. _____

_____

_____

17. Most psychological tests are normative and produce scores that are relative to the performance of others, not some absolute standard. _____

_____

_____

18. In psychological measurement, the average score serves as the reference point and an index of variation is the unit of measurement. _____

_____

19. A psychological test must be reliable. _____

_____

20. Measures of reliability include (a) test-retest _____

_____

    and (b) internal consistency _____

_____

21. A psychological test must be valid. _____

_____

22. Measures of validity include (a) construct validity _____

_____

    and (b) predictive validity _____

_____

23. What are the steps involved in constructing a psychological test? _____

_____

_____

_____

_____

Expanding Your Knowledge and Understanding: Name That Concept

Waiting to meet a student outside her classroom, Dr. White overheard her students talking about a chemistry class they had earlier that day. The students had received their scores for a departmental, comprehensive mid-term test. The test was given to all general chemistry students and was scored by three instructors. The students had much to say about the exam and their scores. Identify the concept about which each student is talking.

1. Bill: "The test was impossible. I did OK on the essay questions...made a C. But those multiple choice questions. They were much more about such little details compared to the other questions. These two sections were not comparable. I flunked the multiple choice questions."

   _____

2. Archie: "Even if I took the test again and again, my grade would be the same -- a lousy C."

   _____

3. James: "I don't think that test assessed my general knowledge about chemistry. I have made an A on every test in that class. And on this review test, I made a D."

   _____

4. Pete: "I know this test seems unfair. But I hear that students who do well on this test do well in the next chemistry course -- organic. And those who don't do well have all sorts of trouble in organic."

   _____

5. Kelsey: "I made an A. I wonder what the average grade was? Did anyone hear?"

   _____

Testing Your Knowledge and Understanding:
Multiple Choice Questions

1. Dr. Estevan is developing a test to assess adolescent shyness. She has a group of adolescents complete the test. A month later the test is administered to the same adolescents. Dr. Estevan is evaluating the test's
   a. face validity
   b. internal consistency
   c. construct validity
   d. test-retest reliability

2. Which student has the best understanding of validity?
    a. Melvin: "Validity means that you get consistent scores."
    b. Helen: "Validity means that the test is internally consistent."
    c. Jack: "Validity means that a test measures what it is supposed to measure."
    d. Stella: "Validity means a test looks appropriate for what it should be measuring."

3. Brendan just took a test that assessed depression. His score on the test was 67. What do you need to know in order to interpret his score?
    a. the unit of measurement used
    b. whether the zero point is true or arbitrary
    c. the average score on the test
    d. his score in retesting

4. Which option does not go with the others?
    a. consistency
    b. validity
    c. reliability
    d. stability

5. _____ is the extent to which a test measures an abstract attribute.
    a. Face validity
    b. Predictive validity
    c. Construct validity
    d. Ipsative validity

6. Meredith just gave a history test that included multiple choice and short answer questions. When she correlated scores on the two parts, she obtained a correlation of .85. She can conclude that the test has
    a. predictive validity
    b. test-retest reliability
    c. internal consistency
    d. construct validity

7. The _____ is used for comparisons of scores on a test.
    a. norm group
    b. validity group
    c. reliability group
    d. ipsative group

8. A norm group for a given test should
    a. be a sample of people drawn from the population for which the test is intended
    b. have several opportunities to take the test so that their best scores can be used
    c. represent the entire population of the United States
    d. be changed each year

Applying Your Knowledge and Understanding: Challenge

Dr. O'Brien has spent several years developing a new assessment measure of intelligence in adults. He has determined that shoe size is predictive of intelligence. Specifically, more intelligent people have small feet and less intelligent people have big feet. The theory behind this measure is quite simple. Given that the body has only so much energy to use, when the energy is being spent on growing big feet, there is less energy for brain growth and development. Similarly, when the body's energy is serving brain growth and development, there is less energy for foot growth.

The assessment consisted of measuring the person's foot -- from heel to toe -- to determine shoe size, then using the formula below to determine the person's intelligence.

$$1 / \text{shoe size} \times 1000$$

1. Is this measure reliable? _____

_____

_____

2. Is this test valid? _____

_____

_____

3. Can a test be reliable but not valid? _____

_____

_____

_____

4. Can a test be valid but not reliable? _____

_____

_____

ANSWERS

Name That Concept

1. internal consistency
2. test-retest reliability
3. validity
4. predictive validity
5. norms

Multiple Choice

1. d	5. c
2. c	6. c
3. c	7. a
4. b	8. a

Chapter 31 -- Behavior Can Be Predicted from Personality Measures--But Imperfectly

(or Why Personality Is Best Thought of As an Interaction Between Traits and Situations)

Checking Your Knowledge: Terms, Statements, & Questions

After you have read this chapter, you should be able to define the terms/concepts, explain the statements, and answer the questions in this section *in your own words*. When appropriate, it may help to give a concrete example of the term or statement. It is most helpful if you try to answer in your own words before looking in the textbook.

1. facet _____

_____

2. five-factor model of personality (the "Big 5") _____

_____

3. personality _____

_____

4. phenomenology _____

_____

5. projective techniques _____

_____

6. self-report questionnaires _____

_____

7. Psychological testing assumes consistency within a person and consistent differences between

people. _____

8. Two goals of personality assessment are understanding and prediction. _____

_____

_____

9. When do psychologists use factor analysis? _____

_____

_____

10. Describe the basic process of factor analysis. How can you tell if any given test (or as in the

example in the text, any given personality scale) should be considered part of a larger factor?

_____

_____

_____

_____

11. How are personality tests used in job placement? _____

_____

_____

12. What did Walter Mischel mean when he proposed that we should define situations in terms of

their psychologically relevant characteristics, then look across situations for similarity in terms

of those psychological features? _____

_____

_____

_____

Testing Your Knowledge and Understanding:
Multiple Choice Questions

1. Many psychologists have raised concerns about the reliability and validity of which of the following personality assessment techniques?
   a. self-report questionnaires
   b. California Personality Inventories
   c. projective tests
   d. Hogan Personality Inventories

2. Which of the following global factors is not considered one of the "Big 5"?
   a. agreeableness
   b. extroversion
   c. openness to experience
   d. altruism

3. Wendy recently took a personality test and found out she scored very high on a scale of extroversion. Which of the following is the best way to interpret this result?
   a. Wendy is probably extroverted in many circumstances, but won't be extroverted in every situation she's in.
   b. Wendy is probably extroverted in every interaction she has with another person.
   c. Wendy's score is meaningless, because a personality test can't reveal anything about her.
   d. Wendy is probably really shy, and the test isn't at all accurate.

4. Personality is best thought of as an interaction between
   a. situations and evolutionary advances
   b. situations and parental influence
   c. traits and situations
   d. traits and character

Applying Your Knowledge and Understanding:
Challenge

1. Have you ever taken any type of personality test? What did it reveal about you? Even if you have never taken a personality test, how do you suppose you would fare relative to each of the Big 5?

2. What do you think of Mischel's theory that personality should be defined in terms of an interaction between traits and situations? Regarding the expression of an individual's personality, do you agree that the psychological characteristics of a situation are more important than the nominal characteristics (defined by name, such as situations in class, or at home, or at summer camp)? Can you think of any examples of how personality traits of you or someone you know were expressed similarly across different situations that may have had similar psychological characteristics?

ANSWERS

Multiple Choice

1. c
2. d
3. a
4. c

Chapter 32 -- Intellectual Ability Has a Substantial Impact on Many Aspects of People's Lives

(or Why Not Everybody Can Be a Rocket Scientist)

Checking Your Knowledge:
Terms, Statements, & Questions

After you have read this chapter, you should be able to define the terms/concepts, explain the statements, and answer the questions in this section *in your own words*. When appropriate, it may help to give a concrete example of the term or statement. It is most helpful if you try to answer in your own words before looking in the textbook.

1. Flynn effect _____

_____

2. Intelligence Quotient _____

_____

3. mental age _____

_____

4. normal curve _____

_____

5. normal distribution _____

_____

6. Intelligence Quotient (IQ) refers to performance on an intelligence test and has meaning only in

relation to other test scores. _____

_____

7. IQ is normally distributed with a mean score of 100. _____

_____

8. Intelligence tests are highly reliable. _____

_____

9. Generalizations about the relationship of IQ to other aspects of behavior are based on group data and there are individual exceptions. _____

_____

10. What are the properties of a normal distribution of IQ scores? _____

_____

_____

11. Why are scores from intelligence tests for adults not truly intelligence "quotients?" Why do we still call them IQs? _____

_____

_____

Expanding Your Knowledge and Understanding: Normal Distributions

1. What other human characteristics are most likely distributed normally? _____

_____

_____

_____

_____

2. What is the advantage of a normal distribution over other distributions? _____

_____

_____

_____

_____

Testing Your Knowledge and Understanding: Multiple Choice Questions

1. Which student has the correct understanding of the distribution of IQ scores?
   a. Kara: "It is triangular, with the most at 100."
   b. Sondra: "Separate distributions are necessary for women and men."
   c. Jonas: "The distribution is bell-shaped."
   d. Cal: "The shape of the distribution depends upon the age of people tested."

2. If Rebecca scored a mental age of 10 on an intelligence test, she
   a. is 8 years old
   b. can answer the number of questions answered by the typical 10-year-old
   c. has a potential to perform at the level of the typical 9-year-old
   d. has an average IQ

3. Prior to Binet, intelligence had been considered a _____ construct
   a. cognitive
   b. social
   c. sensory
   d. concrete

4. Which student identified one of Binet's key contributions to intelligence testing?
   a. Sam: "He defined intelligence in terms of sensory-motor abilities."
   b. Ted: "He created the concept of IQ."
   c. Mabel: "He created the concept of validity."
   d. Marvin: "He developed a test in which item difficulty was tied to age of test taker."

5. Historically, IQ was defined as
   a. (chronological age / mental age) x 100
   b. (chronological age x mental age) / 100
   c. (mental age / chronological age) x 100
   d. (mental age x 100) / chronological age

Applying Your Knowledge and Understanding: Challenges

1. After taking General Psychology, Susan wants to take an IQ test and find out what her IQ is. What are the pros and cons of doing so?

2. Anthony thinks his son could be doing better in school. To verify his belief, he calls a psychologist so his son can take an IQ test. Anthony is confident that when he has "proof" that his son is very intelligent and he tells his son this, then his son will begin applying himself in school. Anthony stresses how important this is since he can't afford to send all nine of his children to school and he was certain that his son was bright enough to win a full scholarship.

(a) Do you think Anthony's son should be tested? Explain your answer. _____

_____

_____

_____

_____

(b) Should Anthony and his son be told the son's IQ? What are the pros and cons of doing so?

_____

_____

_____

_____

_____

(c) What social psychology concepts that you have already learned in this course impact the

pros and cons of telling someone what his or her IQ is? _____

_____

_____

_____

_____

ANSWERS

Multiple Choice

1. c
2. b
3. c
4. d
5. c

Chapter 33 -- Many Individual Differences Have a Strong Genetic Component

(or Why Identical Twins Behave More Similarly Than Do Fraternal Twins)

Checking Your Knowledge:
Terms, Statements, & Questions

After you have read this chapter, you should be able to define the terms/concepts, explain the statements, and answer the questions in this section *in your own words*. When appropriate, it may help to give a concrete example of the term or statement. It is most helpful if you try to answer in your own words before looking in the textbook.

1. concordance rate _____

_____

2. heritability index _____

_____

3. monozygotic twins _____

_____

4. Intelligence has a substantial genetic component, as indicated by heritability indices. _____

_____

_____

5. Some personality traits have a genetic component, as indicated by heritability indices. _____

_____

_____

6. Schizophrenia has a substantial genetic component, as indicated by concordance rates. _____

_____

_____

7. Sexual orientation may have a genetic component, as indicated by concordance rates. _____

_____

_____

8. Both heredity and environment influence all psychological individual differences. _____

_____

_____

9. In the area of investigating individual differences, why is "nature vs. nurture" the wrong way to ask the question of underlying causal factors? _____

_____

_____

10. Does the fact that there are group differences in the average IQ scores among African Americans, White Americans, and Asian Americans support the argument that there are genetic differences with regard to intelligence? Why or why not? _____

_____

_____

_____

_____

11. What did you learn in Part 9 (chapters 30, 31, 32, and 33) that supports the Basic Idea that "human beings differ *dramatically* from each other. These differences arise from a combination of environmental and genetic factors?" _____

_____

_____

_____

_____

12. What did you learn in Part 9 that supports the Basic Idea that *"much* human behavior results from an interaction between past experience and the immediate situation?" _____

_____

_____

_____

_____

13. What did you learn in Part 9 that supports the Basic Idea that "you cannot understand psychology without understanding evolution. Behavior results from an interaction between genetic factors and the immediate situation?" _____

_____

_____

_____

_____

_____

Expanding Your Knowledge and Understanding: Measurements

How do heritability indices and concordance rates differ from each other?

_____

_____

_____

_____

_____

_____

Testing Your Knowledge and Understanding:
Multiple Choice Questions

1. Which student is most accurate in summarizing the genetic component of schizophrenia?
   a. Cheryl: "Genetics has been found to be *the* critical factor."
   b. Katie: "A potential for schizophrenia may be inherited."
   c. Morgan: "If one identical twin is schizophrenic, the other twin will be at some time."
   d. Caitlin: "Children of a schizophrenic father will develop schizophrenia."

2. If genetic differences were _____ and environment differences were _____, the heritability indices would be higher.
   a. reduced; reduced
   b. held constant; reduced
   c. reduced; held constant
   d. reduced; increased

3. Which individual is most likely to develop schizophrenia?
   a. Ralph, whose cousin was diagnosed as schizophrenic when Ralph was 6
   b. Al, whose younger sister was diagnosed as schizophrenic when Al was 22
   c. Jill, whose half-sister was diagnosed as schizophrenic when Jill was 18
   d. Madge, whose fraternal twin was diagnosed as schizophrenic when Madge was 30

4. If you were going to conduct a study to investigate the relative contribution of genetics and environment to intelligence, which design should you use?
   a. compare the IQs of fraternal twins and monozygotic twins reared together
   b. compare the IQs of fraternal twins reared together with monozygotic twins reared apart
   c. compare the IQs of fraternal twins reared together with the IQs of fraternal twins reared apart
   d. compare the IQs of monozygotic twins reared apart with the IQs of monozygotic twins reared together

5. Which student offered the best understanding of the causes of schizophrenia?
   a. Janice: "Schizophrenia is entirely genetically based."
   b. Emily: "Some environmental factors are necessary to trigger the development of schizophrenia in those who have a genetic predisposition."
   c. Stan: "Although there can be a small environmental factor, the cause is 90% genetic."
   d. Melanie: "We really don't have much information about the causes of schizophrenia."

Applying Your Knowledge and Understanding: Challenge

Some psychologists propose that heredity may impose lower and upper limits on intelligence and that environment determines an individual's place within these limits. The home environment is believed to be a critical factor in the environmental contribution to intelligence. What kind of home environment do you believe would nurture intellectual development?

_____

_____

_____

_____

_____

_____

_____

ANSWERS

Multiple Choice

1. b
2. b
3. d
4. d
5. b

Chapter 34 -- Emotions, Like Thoughts, Arise in the Brain

(or Why You Get Goose Bumps)

Checking Your Knowledge:
Terms, Statements, & Questions

After you have read this chapter, you should be able to define the terms/concepts, explain the statements, and answer the questions in this section *in your own words*. When appropriate, it may help to give a concrete example of the term or statement. It is most helpful if you try to answer in your own words before looking in the textbook.

1. arousal response _____

_____

2. fight-or-flight response _____

_____

3. visceral response _____

_____

4. There are cross-species similarities in emotional displays. _____

_____

_____

5. There are cross-cultural similarities in emotional displays. _____

_____

_____

6. Different emotions arise from specific brain circuits. _____

_____

_____

7. Explain William James' theory of emotion. _____

_____

_____

8. What are the problems with James' theory? _____

_____

_____

9. What is Cannon's theory of emotion? _____

_____

_____

10. What are the problems with Cannon's theory? _____

_____

_____

Expanding Your Knowledge and Understanding: Physiology and Emotions

1. Explain how our physiological response and emotional response interplay in the fight-or-flight response. What would happen, for example, the very moment you saw a bear in the woods?

_____

_____

_____

_____

2. What evidence is there for this interplay?

_____

_____

_____

_____

_____

_____

3. How is this interplay evolutionarily fitness-increasing?

_____

_____

_____

_____

_____

_____

Testing Your Knowledge and Understanding:
Multiple Choice Questions

1. While researchers may disagree about the exact number, there appears to be about _____ basic human emotions.
   a. 4
   b. 10
   c. 50
   d. 100

2. When you hear a noise in the woods walking back to your dorm room, the information travels through a direct emotional pathway, from the _____ to the _____, and produces your unconscious physiological response.
   a. thalamus; cerebral cortex
   b. amygdala; thalamus
   c. thalamus; corpus callosum
   d. thalamus; amygdala

3. While your unconscious is responding to the noise in the woods, your conscious brain is also responding. Information goes through an indirect emotional pathway, from the _____ to the _____ to the _____, and you begin to evaluate the situation to decide whether the noise is a real threat.
   a. cortex; amygdala; thalamus
   b. thalamus; cortex; amygdala
   c. thalamus; cortex; corpus callosum
   d. cortex; thalamus; amygdala

Applying Your Knowledge and Understanding:
Scared to Death

There is some anecdotal and (a little) research evidence to show that people can sometimes be, literally, scared to death. That is, with no previous history of health problems, people sometimes die from their physiological response to fear when it is extreme and intense. To quote an example given in Dolnick (1989):

> "On November 19, 1983, Pearl Pizzamiglio, age 60, was working as a hotel clerk when Michael Stewart handed her a paper bag with a note: 'Don't say a word. Put all the money in this bag and no one will get hurt.' Pizzamiglio complied, Stewart fled, and the police were called. Two hours later Pizzamiglio was dead of heart failure. She had had no history of heart trouble and a jury, convinced that Stewart had scared her to death, later convicted him of murder."

1. Why do you suppose some (otherwise healthy) people's response to a fearful situation would kill them, while others' wouldn't?

_____

_____

_____

_____

_____

_____

2. In the above example, do you think the jury was right in convicting Stewart of murder? Why or why not?

_____

_____

_____

_____

_____

_____

ANSWERS

Multiple Choice

1. b
2. d
3. b

REFERENCE

Dolnick, E. (1989, March/April). Scared to death. *Hippocrates*, pp. 106-108.

Chapter 35 -- Stress Can Seriously Affect Your Health

(or Why Driving to Work Every Day Can Kill You, Even If You Never Have an Accident)

Checking Your Knowledge: Terms, Statements, & Questions

After you have read this chapter, you should be able to define the terms/concepts, explain the statements, and answer the questions in this section *in your own words*. When appropriate, it may help to give a concrete example of the term or statement. It is most helpful if you try to answer in your own words before looking in the textbook.

1. autonomic nervous system

   _____

   _____

2. general adaptation syndrome

   _____

   _____

3. parasympathetic nervous system

   _____

   _____

4. stress

   _____

   _____

5. stress-buffering hypothesis

   _____

   _____

6. sympathetic nervous system

   _____

   _____

7. Type A behavior pattern

   _____

   _____

8. Type B behavior pattern

   _____

   _____

9. Stress negatively impacts (a) the heart _____

_____

    and (b) the immune system _____

_____

10. There are individual differences in the response to stress regarding (a) Type A versus Type B

    behavior patterns _____

_____

    and (b) anger and hostility _____

_____

11. Numerous factors mitigate the effects of stress. _____

_____

_____

12. The stress-buffering hypothesis addresses the role of social support when dealing with stress.

    How is it hypothesized to (a) affect the appraisal of a stressful event? _____

_____

_____

    and (b) reduce or eliminate the physiological response to a stressful event? _____

_____

_____

13. From an evolutionary perspective, why are our bodies well-adapted for dealing with occasional

    stress, but poorly adapted for dealing with constant stress? _____

_____

_____

_____

14. Which component of Type A behavior seems to be the one that is most strongly related to a greater risk of developing coronary disease? What evidence is there to support your answer?

_____

_____

_____

_____

_____

Expanding Your Knowledge and Understanding: Good and Bad Stress

1. Usually when we think about stress, we think of negative life events (e.g., loss of a job, death of a friend, speeding tickets). However, stress also accompanies positive life events. For example, winning a lottery, vacations, and Christmas are usually positive events that are also stressful. In addition, not all stressors are major events. Everyday occurrences (e.g., a traffic jam) can be stressful as well.

Identify 10 major negative life events, 10 major positive life events, 10 daily negative events, and 10 daily positive events.

	Major Negative Life Events	Major Positive Life Events	Daily Negative Events	Daily Positive Events
1.	_____	_____	_____	_____
2.	_____	_____	_____	_____
3.	_____	_____	_____	_____
4.	_____	_____	_____	_____
5.	_____	_____	_____	_____
6.	_____	_____	_____	_____
7.	_____	_____	_____	_____
8.	_____	_____	_____	_____

9. _____ _____ _____ _____

10. _____ _____ _____ _____

Now, using a scale of 1 to 100, with 100 being the highest level of stress, rate the level of stress that each event listed above causes you to experience. Are the negative events always given higher ratings or do you view some positive events as very stressful?

_____

_____

_____

_____

_____

2. A cascade of minor stressors may begin with a major stressful life event. Identify minor (or lessor) stressors that may be triggered by each of the two major stressful life events listed below.

Graduating from college	**Getting a divorce**
1. _____	_____
2. _____	_____
3. _____	_____
4. _____	_____
5. _____	_____
6. _____	_____
7. _____	_____
8. _____	_____
9. _____	_____
10. _____	_____

Testing Your Knowledge and Understanding:
Multiple Choice Questions

1. Which man is most likely to develop heart problems?
   a. Josh, who yells at anyone who doesn't do what he wants
   b. Brent, who is very ambitious in his job
   c. David, who is impatient with most people
   d. Will, who is always trying to "beat the clock"

2. Which of the following does not appear to mitigate the effects of stress?
   a. exercise
   b. diet
   c. job satisfaction
   d. denial

3. Chandler is a police officer and father of five. He and his wife share child care. One of their children has chronic health problems and is frequently hospitalized. He has also started law school -- taking one course at a time. Recently, he has experienced frequent indigestion and diarrhea. Chandler would seem to be in the _____ phase of the general adaptation syndrome.
   a. denial
   b. alarm
   c. exhaustion
   d. resistance

4. Who understands the impact stress can have on the immune system?
   a. Amy: "Stress can decrease the activity of the immune system."
   b. Rhonda: "Stress can decrease the activity of the immune system."
   c. Marilyn: "Stress has little effect on the immune system."
   d. Cole: "Low levels of stress can decrease immune system activity temporarily but if the stress continues, the immune system recovers completely."

5. Which aspect of the Type A behavior pattern seems to be most strongly associated with coronary disease?
   a. time urgency
   b. impatience
   c. competitiveness
   d. anger and hostility

6. Which student offered the best discussion of Type A and Type B behavior patterns and illness?
   a. Sylvia: "Angry and hostile Type A people are more likely to develop heart disease than are time-conscious and ambitious Type A people."
   b. Walt: "Type B people are more likely to develop heart disease than are Type A people."
   c. Doug: "Type B and Type A are equally likely to experience cancer but not heart disease."
   d. Sharon: "Research now shows that there is really little difference in the behavior patterns of Type A and Type B people."

7. If Maria has a Type B behavior pattern, she probably
   a. talks very fast
   b. handles stress very well
   c. is likely to have a heart attack
   d. is very time-conscious

8. Which individual is most likely a Type B personality?
   a. Eric, and angry and irritable college professor
   b. Chip, a self-confident, hard-driven actor
   c. Camille, an easy-going, relaxed stockbroker
   d. Jack, a hard-driving, time-conscious printer

Applying Your Knowledge and Understanding: Challenge

The role of social support in coping with stress has been acknowledged. How might each situation fit the stress-disease model presented at the end of this chapter? What might be the specific effects of social support in these situations (in light of the model)?

1. A survivor of rape perceives the social support of her family as controlling, but she has found positive support through a therapy group.

_____

_____

_____

_____

_____

_____

2. After working for 20 years at a job he loves, John is fired with no immediate explanation.

_____

_____

_____

ANSWERS

Multiple Choice

1. a   5. d
2. d   6. a
3. c   7. b
4. b   8. c

Chapter 36 -- Happiness Is More Strongly Related to How People Live Their Lives Than to Their Material Circumstances

(or Why Money Doesn't Buy Happiness)

Checking Your Knowledge:
Terms, Statements, & Questions

After you have read this chapter, you should be able to define the terms/concepts, explain the statements, and answer the questions in this section *in your own words*. When appropriate, it may help to give a concrete example of the term or statement. It is most helpful if you try to answer in your own words before looking in the textbook.

1. cross-sectional study _____

_____

2. longitudinal study _____

_____

3. social networks _____

_____

4. People with strong social relationships are happier. _____

_____

_____

5. People who are satisfied with their jobs are happier than those who aren't. _____

_____

_____

6. What variables are *not* related to happiness as strongly as most people probably think they are?

_____

_____

_____

7. What variables *are* related to happiness? _____
_____
_____

8. Describe Csikszentmihalyi's model of job satisfaction. What does he mean by the terms flow, boredom, anxiety, and apathy? How are they related to job satisfaction? _____
_____
_____
_____
_____

9. What role does adaptation play in the finding that "happiness is relative?" _____
_____
_____
_____

10. What did you learn in Part 10 (chapters 34, 35, and 36) that supports the Basic Idea that "you cannot understand psychology without understanding evolution. Behavior results from an interaction between genetic factors and the immediate situation?" _____
_____
_____
_____

11. What did you learn in Part 10 that supports the Basic Idea that "adaptation is *the* fundamental property of human behavior and cognition?" _____
_____
_____
_____

Expanding Your Knowledge and Understanding: Aging and Work

In some countries, people have to retire at the age of 55 and are provided with a guaranteed income for life. What are the pros and cons of such a policy with regard to feelings of happiness?

_____

_____

_____

_____

_____

Expanding Your Knowledge and Understanding: Happiness Is...

There are many common sayings that focus on happiness and its underlying factors. For example, people sometimes say, "You can never be too rich or too thin," and "Money can't buy you happiness."

1. List sayings about feelings of well-being, happiness, life satisfaction, etc. that you have heard.

_____

_____

_____

_____

_____

2. Are there particular themes you see in the sayings you listed? If so, what are they?

_____

_____

_____

_____

_____

_____

3. How do these themes fit with the findings discussed in this chapter?

_____

_____

_____

_____

_____

_____

Testing Your Knowledge and Understanding: Multiple Choice Questions

1. In a _____, groups of people of different ages are compared with one another at a given time.
   a. longitudinal study
   b. cross-sectional study
   c. sequential study
   d. cross-age study

2. If Dr. O'Neill administers her Happy Scale to the same group of people each year for 10 years, she is conducting a _____.
   a. longitudinal study
   b. cross sectional study
   c. sequential study
   d. cross-age study

3. Which of the following is not a determinant of satisfaction with work?
   a. perceived fairness of pay
   b. flow
   c. satisfaction with co-workers
   d. job title

4. Which of the following has not been shown to be related to feelings of well-being?
   a. money
   b. gender
   c. marital status
   d. social network

Applying Your Knowledge and Understanding: Challenge

Are there different types of happiness? For example, is there a state that might fluctuate minute-to-minute and a trait or deeper level of happiness that may have more stability?

1. How might these two types of happiness differ?

_____

_____

_____

_____

_____

2. Do you think that both would have the same underlying factors?

_____

_____

_____

_____

_____

ANSWERS

Multiple Choice

1. b
2. a
3. d
4. b

Chapter 37 -- Psychological Health Means Behaving Appropriately to the Situation

(or Why Most People Function Pretty Well--Most of the Time)

Checking Your Knowledge:
Terms, Statements, & Questions

After you have read this chapter, you should be able to define the terms/concepts, explain the statements, and answer the questions in this section *in your own words*. When appropriate, it may help to give a concrete example of the term or statement. It is most helpful if you try to answer in your own words before looking in the textbook.

1. DSM-IV _____

_____

2. psychopathology _____

_____

3. The behavior of psychologically healthy people is usually appropriate to the situation. _____

_____

_____

4. What is appropriate behavior in a given situation is, in part, culturally defined and can change

over time. _____

_____

5. Describe how each of the following characteristics is relevant to the behavior of psychologically healthy people, as well as how the opposite of each characteristic is manifested in psychologically less healthy people:

(a) productivity _____

_____

_____

(b) the ability to get along with most people _____

_____

_____

(c) a generally good understanding of themselves and how others view them _____

_____

_____

_____

(d) a generally good understanding of the physical world _____

_____

_____

_____

(e) the ability to think clearly and solve problems _____

_____

_____

(f) the ability to focus attention _____

_____

_____

(g) good judgment _____

_____

_____

(h) the ability to experience pleasure _____

_____

_____

(i) the ability to feel strongly about things _____

_____

_____

(j) the ability to give and receive love and affection _____

_____

_____

Expanding Your Knowledge and Understanding: Characteristic Differences

1. Think about the characteristics of psychological health presented in this chapter. Do you think that each characteristic is equally important for men and women? Which might be different, and why?

_____

_____

_____

_____

_____

2. Do you think there are characteristics of psychological health that were not discussed in the text? If so, what are they?

_____

_____

_____

_____

_____

3. How can being a unique individual be a characteristic of both psychological health and psychological illness?

_____

_____

_____

_____

_____

4. Traditional criteria for defining psychopathology include the following:

        statistical infrequency
        violations of social norms
        personal distress
        impairment in functioning
        unexpectedness

How do the characteristics of psychological illness fit with the criteria above?

_____

_____

_____

_____

_____

Applying Your Knowledge and Understanding: Challenges

1. When you first meet someone, what assumptions do you make about that person's psychological health? What factors contribute to your initial impression about his or her psychological health?

_____

_____

_____

_____

_____

_____

2. This chapter listed 10 separate characteristics of psychological health. Does an individual have to possess all 10 to be psychologically healthy? Are 8 enough? Are any of them absolutely mandatory? At what point is the line to "psychologically unhealthy" crossed?

_____

_____

_____

_____

_____

_____

Chapter 38 -- Psychotherapy Can Help Many People Who Behave Inappropriately to the Situation

(or What Classical Conditioning Has to Do with Phobias)

Checking Your Knowledge: Terms, Statements, & Questions

After you have read this chapter, you should be able to define the terms/concepts, explain the statements, and answer the questions in this section *in your own words*. When appropriate, it may help to give a concrete example of the term or statement. It is most helpful if you try to answer in your own words before looking in the textbook.

1. agoraphobia without panic disorder

   _____

   _____

2. clinical psychologist

   _____

   _____

3. generalized anxiety disorder

   _____

   _____

4. obsessive-compulsive disorder

   _____

   _____

5. panic disorder

   _____

   _____

6. panic disorder with agoraphobia

   _____

   _____

7. posttraumatic distress disorder

   _____

   _____

8. psychiatrist

   _____

   _____

9. psychiatric social worker _____

_____

10. psychoanalyst _____

_____

11. systematic
    desensitization _____

_____

12. The majority of mental illnesses suffered by people under the age of 60 are anxiety disorders,

schizophrenia, or affective disorders. _____

_____

13. Anxiety disorders can seriously disrupt a person's life but usually do not require

hospitalization. _____

_____

14. Systematic desensitization is a commonly used treatment for a specific phobia. _____

_____

_____

15. The steps in using systematic desensitization in the treatment of a specific phobia are:

(a) history taking _____

_____

(b) relaxation training _____

_____

(c) construction of an anxiety hierarchy _____

_____

and (d) presentation of hierarchy items during states of relaxation _____

_____

16. What are the different types of talk therapy? _____

_____   _____

_____

17. What is the difference between an efficacy study and an effectiveness study? Which type is

better when trying to evaluate talk therapy, and why? _____

_____

_____

_____

_____

Testing Your Knowledge and Understanding: Multiple Choice Questions

1. Psychiatrists and clinical psychologists are alike in that
   a. both are MDs
   b. both prescribe drugs
   c. both are psychoanalysts
   d. both treat psychopathology

2. Which of the following is not an anxiety disorder?
   a. phobia
   b. posttraumatic distress disorder
   c. dementia
   d. panic disorder

3. Agoraphobia is a fear of
   a. heights
   b. the dark
   c. open spaces
   d. tight places -- like closets

4. How do a generalized anxiety disorder and a specific phobia differ?
   a. A specific phobia focuses on only one object whereas generalized anxiety disorder focuses on at least three specific objects.
   b. Generalized anxiety disorder seems to be learned whereas a phobia is due to unconscious instinctual urges.
   c. The anxiety is situationally caused in specific phobia but not in generalized anxiety disorder.
   d. A specific phobia is more difficult to treat.

5. Systematic desensitization is a treatment for
   a. generalized anxiety disorder
   b. panic disorder without agoraphobia
   c. obsessive-compulsive disorder
   d. specific phobia

6. In what way does a fear and a phobia differ?
   a. A fear is specific and a phobia is general.
   b. A phobia is specific and a fear is general.
   c. A fear is irrational and a phobia is rational.
   d. A phobia is irrational and a fear is rational.

7. Compared to panic disorders, generalized anxiety disorder
   a. always has higher levels of anxiety
   b. is less chronic
   c. is generally milder with regard to the highest levels of anxiety
   d. has more powerful physical symptoms

8. When Jenna walks down the street, she's very careful to avoid stepping on cracks. When stopped at a railroad crossing, she has to count the train cars. After she vacuums, she spends hours combing out the fringe on the rugs. Jenna probably suffers from
   a. generalized anxiety disorder
   b. obsessive-compulsive disorder
   c. posttraumatic distress disorder
   d. panic disorder

Applying Your Knowledge and Understanding:
Identify the Anxiety Disorder

See if you can identify which anxiety disorders are described below.

_____ 1. Tom complains of continuous worries and fears about seemingly everything. He has trouble concentrating, is irritable, and has trouble sleeping. He has felt this way for about a year.

_____ 2. Heather is terrified of the dark. She has multiple lights in each room and refuses to enter a room if any light has burned out.

_____ 3. Jennifer goes only to the property line around her house. She is terrified to go any further away from home and, in fact, has missed all of her son's basketball games.

_____ 4. Brad cannot go through a day without washing his hands at least 100 times.

_____ 5. Parker was one of two survivors of a plane crash. Two years later, he keeps re-experiencing the crash. He used to live by an airport but moved to a small town with no airport to avoid hearing jets landing.

_____ 6. Lucy reported that one day she was driving home from school, thinking about nothing in particular. Then, out of the blue, she was filled with terror -- her heart was pounding and she could not breathe. She was convinced that she was going to die. Then it went away. This is the third time this has happened to her recently.

ANSWERS

Multiple Choice

1. d	5. d
2. c	6. d
3. c	7. c
4. c	8. b

Identify the Anxiety Disorder

1. generalized anxiety disorder
2. specific phobia (specifically, nyctophobia)
3. agoraphobia without panic disorder
4. obsessive-compulsive disorder
5. posttraumatic distress disorder
6. panic disorder

Chapter 39 -- Schizophrenia, the Most Serious Form of Mental Illness, Is a Brain Disease

(or Why There Are Many Fewer Patients in Mental Hospitals Today Than There Were in 1960)

Checking Your Knowledge:
Terms, Statements, & Questions

After you have read this chapter, you should be able to define the terms/concepts, explain the statements, and answer the questions in this section *in your own words*. When appropriate, it may help to give a concrete example of the term or statement. It is most helpful if you try to answer in your own words before looking in the textbook.

1. chlorpromazine _____

_____

2. dopamine _____

_____

3. dopamine hypothesis _____

_____

4. Parkinson's disease _____

_____

5. schizophrenia _____

_____

6. Thorazine _____

_____

7. Schizophrenia is diagnosed by its symptoms; there is no absolute test for it. _____

_____

_____

8. Schizophrenia is a brain disease. _____

9. There is a genetic component to schizophrenia. _____

_____

_____

10. Environmental stress is also a component in the development of schizophrenia. _____

_____

_____

11. Is schizophrenia the same thing as having multiple personalities? _____

_____

_____

12. How is dopamine related to schizophrenia? _____

_____

_____

13. How do anti-schizophrenic drugs work, according to the dopamine hypothesis? _____

_____

_____

Expanding Your Knowledge and Understanding: Name the Symptom

Identify which symptom of schizophrenia is illustrated in each case below. Choose from among the following: affective flattening, catatonic behavior, delusion, disorganized emotionality, disorganized speech, and hallucination.

_____   1. Marla believes that she is Joan of Arc.

_____   2. Kent assumes unusual postures (such as his arms extended out from his shoulders and his head thrown back) and maintains the positions for hours at a time.

_____ 3. Phil believes that his neighbors are stealing his thoughts and inserting other thoughts.

_____ 4. When asked how her day went, Catherine said, "Fine like wine...do you want to dine...my age is nine...and I like pine...the day is long...I know a song...like ping pong...it goes ding dong."

_____ 5. Since George believes he is the President of the United States, he insists that his wife hum "Hail to the Chief" whenever he enters the room.

_____ 6. Faith hears the furniture in her house talk to her.

_____ 7. Marty feels bugs crawling in his brain.

Testing Your Knowledge and Understanding: Multiple Choice Questions

1. _____ is the percentage of close relatives manifesting the same disorder.
   a. Heritability rate
   b. Correlation means
   c. Concordance rate
   d. Genetic rate

2. Dominic hears voices saying things that no one else hears. Dominic is having a(n)
   a. delusion
   b. hallucination
   c. illusion
   d. catatonic allusion

3. Rudy's belief that he is John Travolta is a(n)
   a. delusion
   b. illusion
   c. hallucination
   d. obsession

4. The dopamine hypothesis predicts that if a schizophrenic were given _____, then his symptoms would get _____.
   a. L-DOPA; worse
   b. L-DOPA; better
   c. Phenothiazine; worse
   d. alcohol; better

5. Which of the following is not a risk factor for schizophrenia?
   a. being separated from parents
   b. growing up in a family where there is intense emotional expression
   c. having had birth complications
   d. being born in late spring in the northern hemisphere

6. Which of the following is a drug used in the treatment of schizophrenia?
   a. L-DOPA
   b. Lithium
   c. Dopamine
   d. Thorazine

7. Which student misunderstands schizophrenia?
   a. Anne: "Schizophrenics may have positive or negative symptoms."
   b. Heidi: "There is a genetic basis for a predisposition for schizophrenia."
   c. Bobby: "Almost anyone exposed to very high levels of environmental stress will develop schizophrenia."
   d. Diane: "In some schizophrenia, there seems to be a problem related to dopamine."

Applying Your Knowledge and Understanding: Challenge

Schizophrenia has historically been classified as a mental illness with psychological causes and it has been accompanied by a very large stigma. The individual was treated as if he or she was personally responsible for developing the disease. More recently, as is indicated in the title of this chapter, schizophrenia has been identified as a brain disease -- a medical condition.

1. What are the implications of this "reclassification" of schizophrenia to a medical condition for:

   (a) a person seeking treatment for schizophrenia? _____

   _____

   _____

   _____

   _____

(b) the stigma accompanying schizophrenia for the diagnosed individual? _____

_____

_____

_____

_____

(c) the stigma for the family of the diagnosed individual? _____

_____

_____

_____

_____

(d) the general perception of the disorder? _____

_____

_____

_____

_____

2. Do you think there is still a stigma of "mental illness" attached to schizophrenia in our society, or have most people tended to accept the fact that it is a medical condition? Why might it be difficult for some people to accept the medical explanation and treat schizophrenia as such?

_____

_____

_____

_____

_____

ANSWERS

Name the Symptom

1. delusion
2. catatonic behavior
3. delusion
4. disorganized speech
5. delusion
6. hallucination
7. hallucination

Multiple Choice

1. c
2. b
3. a
4. a
5. d
6. d
7. c

Chapter 40 -- Mood Disorders, the Most Common Form of Severe Mental Illness, Are Highly Treatable

(or What Abraham Lincoln and Georgia O'Keeffe Had in Common)

Checking Your Knowledge: Terms, Statements, & Questions

After you have read this chapter, you should be able to define the terms/concepts, explain the statements, and answer the questions in this section *in your own words*. When appropriate, it may help to give a concrete example of the term or statement. It is most helpful if you try to answer in your own words before looking in the textbook.

1. cognitive therapy   _____

    _____

2. learned helplessness   _____

    _____

3. lithium   _____

    _____

4. major depression   _____

    _____

5. manic depression   _____

    _____

6. MAO inhibitors   _____

    _____

7. mood disorder   _____

    _____

8. SSRI   _____

    _____

9. tricyclics _____

_____

10. Mood disorders are the most common form of serious mental illness. _____

_____

_____

11. Although less common than major depression, manic depression may be more disruptive.

_____

_____

12. Mood disorders are serious risk factors for suicide. _____

_____

_____

13. Mood disorders have a genetic component. _____

_____

_____

14. Environmental factors are also important in the development of mood disorders. _____

_____

_____

15. There is a link between learned helplessness and major depression. _____

_____

_____

16. How is attributional style related to depression? _____

_____

_____

17. What did you learn in Part 11 (chapters 37, 38, 39, and 40) that supports the Basic Idea that "adaptation is *the* fundamental property of human behavior and cognition?" _____

_____

_____

_____

18. What did you learn in Part 11 that supports the Basic Idea that "psychological disorders are primarily brain diseases?" _____

_____

_____

_____

Expanding Your Knowledge and Understanding: Depression and Gender

1. Gender differences are routinely found in the incidence of major depression -- more women than men are given the diagnosis of major depression. What factors do you think may underlie this gender difference?

_____

_____

_____

_____

_____

2. Why do you think there is not a similar gender difference in the diagnosis of manic depression?

_____

_____

_____

_____
_____
_____

_____

Testing Your Knowledge and Understanding:
Multiple Choice Questions

1. Which student has an erroneous understanding of major depression?
   a. Bette: "About 4% of adults are having a major depressive episode at any given time."
   b. Jason: "Men and women suffer equally from major depression."
   c. Barry: "DSM-IV symptoms must be experienced for at least two months."
   d. Ken: "15% of people will have major depression at least once in their lives."

2. Blaming your poor evaluation at work on your own lack of abilities is which type of attribution?
   a. internal, stable
   b. external, stable
   c. external, unstable
   d. internal, unstable

3. Which of the following is not a drug treatment for major depression?
   a. MAO inhibitors
   b. tricyclics
   c. SSRIs
   d. Thorazine

4. What is the treatment of choice for manic depression?
   a. MAO inhibitors
   b. lithium
   c. SSRIs
   d. tricyclics

5. Which drug prevents the re-uptake of serotonin?
   a. tricyclics
   b. MAO inhibitors
   c. neuroleptics
   d. lithium

6. Trudy tells you that no matter how much or how hard she studies, she just can't pass statistics, and there's nothing she can do to change that. She might be experiencing
   a. major depression
   b. delusions of effort
   c. manic depression
   d. learned helplessness

7. Ron doesn't seem to want to do anything. He says nothing gives him pleasure. He feels sad and just wants to sleep. He has trouble thinking and has no energy. This has gone on since his dog died two weeks ago. It appears that
   a. Ron has major depression
   b. Ron is manic depressive
   c. Ron may feel bad but it is probably not major depression
   d. Ron is in a pre-manic state

8. Hamilton has been prescribed medication by a psychiatrist to treat his major depression. The psychiatrist probably believes that Hamilton's depression is due to
   a. a positive feedback loop between depression and attributional style
   b. learned helplessness
   c. inappropriate levels of neurotransmitters in Hamilton's brain
   d. elevated self-esteem

9. Which of the following is not a characteristic of a manic episode?
   a. increased talkativeness
   b. prolonged span of attention
   c. racing thoughts
   d. feelings of grandiosity

Applying Your Knowledge and Understanding: Challenge

Dr. Feelgood, a leading expert on mood disorders, was a guest on Oprah's talk show. The topic was "Psychological (Rather than Medical) Problems of Humans and Their Pets." Dr. Feelgood was quite unhappy about being on this panel. When he was introduced, he apologized to Oprah and explained that his inclusion on this panel was a big mistake. "After all, mood disorders are not strictly psychological problems. Indeed, mood disorders are medical problems that require medical treatment. Medical problems...medical treatment."

1. What is the evidence for this claim (just for humans, not pets)?

_____

_____

_____

_____

2. What is the evidence contrary to this claim?

_____

_____

_____

_____

_____

3. Given your answers to #1 and #2, what is the best approach to treatment?

_____

_____

_____

_____

_____

ANSWERS

Depression and Gender

1. Biological differences and therapist bias in the making of diagnoses have not been found to explain the gender differences. Factors that are hypothesized to underlie the gender differences include: women report experiencing less gratification in their lives; women often derive their identity from another person (e.g., husband, kids); women experience more poverty, violence, and relationship problems; and, when depressed, women focus more on the depression than men do.

2. Manic depression has a stronger genetic component than major depression does.

Multiple Choice

1. b
2. a
3. d
4. b
5. a
6. d
7. c
8. c
9. b

Chapter 41 -- People's Beliefs about Why Things Have Happened to Them Can Have a Big Impact on Their Lives

(or Why a Little Optimism Is a Good Thing)

Checking Your Knowledge:
Terms, Statements, & Questions

After you have read this chapter, you should be able to define the terms/concepts, explain the statements, and answer the questions in this section *in your own words*. When appropriate, it may help to give a concrete example of the term or statement. It is most helpful if you try to answer in your own words before looking in the textbook.

1. fundamental attribution error _____

_____

2. positive illusions _____

_____

3. unrealistic optimism _____

_____

4. People tend to make attributions in ways that result in positive illusions. _____

_____

_____

5. People tend to make internal attributions for good outcomes to themselves and external

attributions for bad outcomes. _____

_____

_____

6. People who hold positive illusions are often more successful than people who do not. _____

_____

_____

_____

7. How does someone with a pessimistic attributional style make attributions about a negative outcome? _____

_____

_____

8. How does someone with an optimistic attributional style make attributions about a negative outcome? _____

_____

_____

9. What is the illusion of control? How was it manifested in Langer's study using lottery tickets?

_____

_____

_____

10. Why are positive illusions irrational, yet not necessarily harmful (maybe even having positive consequences)? _____

_____

_____

Expanding Your Knowledge and Understanding: Attribution Types

Place the number of each attribution by a student who failed a chemistry test below in the correct place in the table.

1. I am so sick of chemistry that I couldn't concentrate.
2. College tests always have trick questions that are impossible.
3. The test was on Friday the 13th.
4. I had a horrible headache during the test.
5. I am no good with symbols.
6. There were 13 questions on that test.
7. I am not smart enough to pass any college test.
8. All the chemistry tests in this professor's courses are so unfair.

| | Internal Attributions | | External Attributions | |
	Stable	Unstable	Stable	Unstable
Global	_____	_____	_____	_____
Specific	_____	_____	_____	_____

Expanding Your Knowledge and Understanding: Explanatory Styles and Adaptiveness

1. How might an optimistic explanatory style be evolutionarily adaptive?

_____

_____

_____

_____

_____

2. Is a pessimistic explanatory style evolutionarily adaptive?

_____

_____

_____

_____

_____

3. Can someone train themselves to become optimistic?

_____

_____

_____

_____

_____

Testing Your Knowledge and Understanding:
Multiple Choice Questions

1. Whitney made the highest exam grade in Western Civilization but her roommate, Zoe, made an F on the same test. Zoe complained that "Dr. Mattson is a horrible lecturer who gives impossible tests." Whitney was pleased with her grade because "I really studied hard for it." These comments reflect
   a. people's tendency to assume responsibility for their lives
   b. people's test anxiety
   c. people's tendency to make attributions that promote the self
   d. people's tendency to make attributions that protect others

2. When Diana is confronted with unpleasant events, she maintains her positive attitude. She tells friends, "I know I was not the cause of the event and it probably isn't going to happen again. I know it isn't worth worrying about." Diana's behavior is typical of a(n)
   a. illusion of control
   b. optimistic explanatory style
   c. pessimistic explanatory style
   d. fundamental explanatory style

3. Jan's typical response when something bad happens is, "Things always go wrong -- no matter how hard I try. Things always turn out badly and always will." Jan appears to have
   a. positive illusions
   b. unrealistic pessimism
   c. an optimistic explanatory style
   d. a pessimistic explanatory style

Applying Your Knowledge and Understanding: Challenge

1. How might a pessimistic explanatory style be related to physical health?

   _____

   _____

   _____

   _____

   _____

2. How might an optimistic explanatory style be related to physical health?

   _____

   _____

   _____

   _____

   _____

ANSWERS

Name the Attribution

	Internal Attributions		External Attributions	
	Stable	**Unstable**	**Stable**	**Unstable**
Global	7	4	2	3
Specific	5	1	8	6

Multiple Choice

1. c
2. b
3. d

Chapter 42 -- Expectations Have a Substantial Effect on Behavior

(or Why It's Important to Do Well on the First Quiz)

Checking Your Knowledge:
Terms, Statements, & Questions

After you have read this chapter, you should be able to define the terms/concepts, explain the statements, and answer the questions in this section *in your own words*. When appropriate, it may help to give a concrete example of the term or statement. It is most helpful if you try to answer in your own words before looking in the textbook.

1. expectancy effects _____

_____

2. Hawthorne effect _____

_____

3. illusory correlation _____

_____

4. placebo effects _____

_____

5. self-fulfilling prophecy _____

_____

6. Expectations people have affect their behavior and the behavior of others. _____

_____

_____

7. Expectation effects are found in a broad variety of settings and relationships, including

   (a) business _____

_____

   (b) medical treatment _____

_____

(c) schools _____

_____

and (d) clinical psychology settings _____

_____

8. How is a self-fulfilling prophecy an example of a positive feedback loop? _____

_____

_____

9. Give an example of a self-fulfilling prophecy, other than the one in the text about expecting your

friend's husband to dislike you, that is likely to be unstable and end up "crashing." _____

_____

_____

_____

10. What is the general conclusion the authors draw about expectancy effects in the classroom?

What evidence supports that conclusion? _____

_____

_____

_____

11. What happened when Rosenhan and the other "pseudopatients" were admitted to psychiatric

hospitals? What did the hospital staff expect to see in them? How did they interpret the

"patients'" behavior in light of those expectations? _____

_____

_____

_____

_____

Expanding Your Knowledge and Understanding:
Related Concepts

1. How is the self-fulfilling prophecy a by-product of the primacy effect?

_____

_____

_____

_____

_____

2. How might illusory correlation and confirmation bias be related?

_____

_____

_____

_____

_____

Testing Your Knowledge and Understanding:
Multiple Choice Questions

1. Rex just met his new boss -- Stephanie. He thought she was pushy, insensitive, and callous. That night he told his wife that all female bosses were pushy, insensitive, and callous. This is an example of a(n)
   a. self-fulfilling prophecy
   b. illusory correlation
   c. expectancy effect
   d. positive feedback loop

2. Margaret thinks that Southerners are incredibly polite. If this particular belief is an illusory correlation, Margaret is likely to
   a. be an accurate assessor of politeness
   b. underestimate the politeness of Southerners
   c. overestimate the politeness of Southerners
   d. assume that non-Southerners are impolite

3. A new boss has been hired at Tires-R-Us. He has a reputation of being a real ogre at his last job. However, Vinnie is convinced that the new boss will be fair and respectful. Much to everyone's surprise, the boss has begun to be fair and respectful. The boss's behavior may reflect
   a. conformity
   b. a self-fulfilling prophecy
   c. an illusory correlation
   d. good humor practices

4. Why are placebos given in drug experiments?
   a. to control for suggestion and expectations
   b. to take the place of random sampling
   c. to take the place of random assignment
   d. to control drug side effects

Applying Your Knowledge and Understanding: Challenges

1. Two clinical psychologists are viewing a videotape in which a highly controversial assessment technique was used. When asked about their responses to the tape, Psychologist A said, "I wouldn't have believed it if I had not seen it." Psychologist B said, "I wouldn't have seen it if I did not believe it." Explain their comments in terms of people's expectations.

_____

_____

_____

_____

_____

2. What research participant expectations may affect that participant's behavior? Have you had any prior expectations in any research you've participated in for this class? Did it affect you as you completed the study?

_____

_____

_____

_____

_____

3. In a therapy setting, how might the self-fulfilling prophecy, therapist expectations, placebo effects, and client expectations interact?

_____

_____

_____

_____

_____

_____

ANSWERS

Multiple Choice

1. b
2. c
3. b
4. a

Chapter 43 -- Good Decision Making Requires Knowing the World and Knowing Yourself

(or How to Look Before You Leap)

Checking Your Knowledge:
Terms, Statements, & Questions

After you have read this chapter, you should be able to define the terms/concepts, explain the statements, and answer the questions in this section *in your own words*. When appropriate, it may help to give a concrete example of the term or statement. It is most helpful if you try to answer in your own words before looking in the textbook.

1. balance sheet _____

_____

2. decision aids _____

_____

3. descriptive decision model _____

_____

4. Expected Value model _____

_____

5. framing effect _____

_____

6. normative decision model _____

_____

7. prescriptive decision
   model _____

_____

8. sunk costs _____

_____

9. utility _____

_____

10. Problem solving often involves the decision aids of externalization and decomposition. _____

_____

_____

11. According to the Expected Value model, a normative account of decision making, a decision

should maximize the expected value of the outcome. _____

_____

_____

12. Key elements of the Expected Value model are (a) the set of choice options _____

_____

_____

(b) the set of possible states of the world _____

_____

_____

(c) the probability of each outcome _____

_____

_____

and (d) the costs and payoffs associated with each possible outcome _____

_____

_____

13. Useful principles in decision making are (a) remembering that optimal decision making

requires that facts and values be kept independent _____

_____

_____

_____

and (b) knowing that the outcome of a decision will not let a person determine if the right

decision was made _____

_____

_____

14. The balance sheet is a nonmathematical prescriptive decision aid with three critical distinctions:

(a) utilitarian consequences versus anticipated approval or disapproval _____

_____

_____

(b) consequences for self versus others _____

_____

_____

and (c) positive versus negative anticipated consequences _____

_____

_____

15. Deviations from good decision making include (a) producing relatively few decision options

_____

_____

(b) not considering enough possible states of the world _____

_____

_____

(c) allowing utilities assessment to be affected by the measurement instrument _____

_____

and (d) being influenced by sunk costs _____

_____

16. How do people deviate from the normative model at each of the decision elements of the

Expected Value model? _____

_____

_____

17. What other problems do people often have with aspects of decision making? _____

_____

_____

18. What are the steps in Janis & Mann's prescriptive model of decision making? _____

_____

_____

19. What are the advantages to using a balance sheet when making an important decision? _____

_____

_____

_____

_____

Expanding Your Knowledge and Understanding:
Irrational Behavior?

Ray pays $600 each year for homeowner's insurance and hopes he will never have to file a claim. Over a 20-year period, Ray will pay $12,000 for the insurance and expects to get none of it back. How can the Expected Value model explain this apparently irrational behavior?

_____

_____

_____

_____

_____

Testing Your Knowledge and Understanding:
Multiple Choice Questions

1. Which of the following is not a major approach to the study of decision making?
   a. descriptive
   b. prescriptive
   c. expective
   d. normative

2. When packing hamburger, a grocer marks the packages as "85% pure ground chuck" instead of "no more than 15% fat." He is showing sensitivity to
   a. framing effects
   b. sunk costs
   c. utilities
   d. status of the world

3. The balance sheet model for decision making is a(n) _____ model.
   a. normative
   b. independent
   c. prescriptive
   d. descriptive

4. _____ is the personal worth of an outcome in decision making.
   a. Choice
   b. Status of the world
   c. Probability value
   d. Utility

Applying Your Knowledge and Understanding: Challenges

1. Think of the last major decision you made (e.g., buying a car). How did your decision making deviate from the elements of normative decision making?

_____

_____

_____

_____

_____

2. Consider the most major decision that is facing you now, or is expected to come up soon (or actually, anytime in the future), such as choosing a major, moving to a new place, buying a car, etc. First, think about the decision options and get an idea of which one you'd likely choose, or are at least leaning toward. Then, use Janis and Mann's balance sheet (you can copy the blank one in your text) to analyze your decision options. Were there any differences in the outcome? Were you able to consider more options and/or consequences when they were on paper instead of in your head?

_____

_____

_____

_____

_____

3. After reading this chapter, you should have a good general understanding of the fact that people very often do not make decisions according to a normative model, and in fact, there are many different ways in which people deviate from optimal decision making. You also know by now, if you've read the first 42 chapters of this book, that one of the Basic Ideas running throughout the book is that evolution has played a major role in getting the human race where it is today -- much human behavior results from an interaction between genetic factors and the immediate situation. How might descriptive (i.e., non-optimal) aspects of decision making -- the way we actually make decisions -- have been selected for? It may not be optimal, but could it be fitness-increasing? Explain your answer.

ANSWERS

Irrational Behavior?

The subjective utility of paying the premiums each year is that Ray is buying a sense of security.

Multiple Choice

1. c
2. a
3. c
4. d

Chapter 44 -- Many Machines Are Harder to Use Than They Ought to Be

(or Who to Blame If You Can't Program Your VCR)

Checking Your Knowledge:
Terms, Statements, & Questions

After you have read this chapter, you should be able to define the terms/concepts, explain the statements, and answer the questions in this section *in your own words*. When appropriate, it may help to give a concrete example of the term or statement. It is most helpful if you try to answer in your own words before looking in the textbook.

1. arbitrary mapping _____

_____

2. conceptual model _____

_____

3. natural mapping _____

_____

4. Machines are more easily used by people when (a) designers use the conceptual model of the

users _____

_____

(b) control information is in the environment _____

_____

_____

(c) control information is meaningful _____

_____

_____

and (d) designers use natural mappings _____

_____

_____

_____

_____

5. How was the author's conceptual model for a VCR different from the VCR designer's

   conceptual model? _____

   _____

   _____

6. What kind of attributions do people tend to make when they fail to use a machine properly?

   How is this different from the attributional style research you learned about in chapter 41?

   _____

   _____

   _____

   _____

7. What did you learn in Part 12 (chapters 41, 42, 43, and 44) that supports the Basic Idea that

   "science is by far the most powerful way the human race has yet devised for understanding the

   world, including, of course, our own behavior?" _____

   _____

   _____

   _____

8. What did you learn in Part 12 that supports the Basic Idea that "humans have the ability to think

   and reason in very powerful ways, but we also have a number of cognitive limitations that lead

   to systematic errors?" _____

   _____

   _____

   _____

9. What did you learn in Part 12 that supports the Basic Idea that "much human behavior is influenced by other people?" _____

_____

_____

_____

10. What did you learn in Part 12 that supports the Basic Idea that "many cognitive limitations can be overcome by using cognitive tools?" _____

_____

_____

_____

Expanding Your Knowledge and Understanding: Problems with VCRs

1. Over the last 20 years or so, what steps have VCR makers taken to

(a) use the same conceptual model as users? _____

_____

_____

_____

(b) have control information in the environment? _____

_____

_____

_____

(c) use meaningful control information? _____

_____

_____

_____

and (d) use natural mapping? _____

_____

_____

_____

2. What recommendations could you make to VCR designers, or to designers of any other machine you may have had difficulty using at one time or another, regarding the above suggestions? Are VCRs generally completely "user-friendly" by this point in their evolution?

_____

_____

_____

_____

_____

_____

_____

_____

Testing Your Knowledge and Understanding:
Multiple Choice Questions

1. Which example suggests that users and designers are using different conceptual models?
    a. using a doorknob that is turned clockwise to open the door
    b. using a door with a horizontal handle that you pull to open the door
    c. using a door with a handle you push down to open the door
    d. using a door that you push to open

2. What is Colin most likely to say when he can't make a copy of a tape on a friend's tape player?
   a. "This machine must be broken since it won't copy the tape."
   b. "This is really a dumb machine -- it is impossible to work."
   c. "This machine makes me realize how really dumb I am."
   d. "I bet no one can copy this tape using this machine."

3. Which is not a human-machine interaction problem?
   a. Machine designers use a conceptual model that differs from that of the users.
   b. Machine designers incorporate control information in the machine.
   c. Machine designers use arbitrary control information.
   d. Machine designers use arbitrary mapping.

Applying Your Knowledge and Understanding: Challenges

1. Books were identified by the authors as perfect "machines" that are commonly in use. What other perfect "machines" can you identify? What makes them perfect?

_____

_____

_____

_____

_____

2. The authors also mentioned the difficulties with the punch card ballot used in parts of Florida during the 2000 presidential election.

   (a) Compare and contrast the design of the punch card ballot (see picture in text) with the suggestions for better human-machine interaction presented in this chapter.

_____

_____

_____

_____

_____

(b) Other voting machines and systems around the country have also posed problems. In every election, there are consistently a number of ballots that must be thrown out in every county of every state. If you were given the task of designing one voting system to be implemented throughout the country (and money is no object), what would you design? Do you think there even *could* be just one system/machine that everyone who votes could easily use, that would minimize the number of votes thrown out?

_____

_____

_____

_____

_____

_____

ANSWERS

Multiple Choice

1. b
2. c
3. b

Epilogue -- Psychology and Human Values

Checking Your Knowledge:
Terms, Statements, & Questions

After you have read the epilogue, you should be able to define the terms/concepts, explain the statements, and answer the questions in this section *in your own words*. When appropriate, it may help to give a concrete example of the term or statement. It is most helpful if you try to answer in your own words before looking in the textbook.

1. determinism _____

_____

2. fact _____

_____

3. social constructionism _____

_____

4. value _____

_____

5. Physical reality is knowable. _____

_____

6. Although different from one another, facts and values are not unrelated. _____

_____

_____

7. What we know about reward and punishment should influence the way we treat children.

_____

_____

8. What we know about memory should influence the way we think about education. _____

_____

_____

9. What we know about mental illness should influence the way we treat the mentally ill. _____ _

_____

_____

10. What we know about social influence should help us resist pressures to violate our own

values. _____

_____

11. Knowing some simple techniques can help us make better life decisions. _____

_____

_____

12. Intuitive judgments having to do with numbers are often wrong. _____

_____

13. How does the example given in the text of decision making regarding a person accused of

murder illustrate the concepts of (a) irreducible uncertainty? _____

_____

_____

(b) inevitable error? _____

_____

_____

and (c) unavoidable injustice? _____

_____

_____

Applying Your Knowledge and Understanding:
Challenge

1. What facts presented in this text were consistent with values you hold?

Value	Fact

1. What facts presented in this text challenged values you hold?

Value	Fact
_____	_____
	_____
	_____
_____	_____
	_____
	_____
_____	_____
	_____
	_____
_____	_____
	_____
	_____
_____	_____
	_____
	_____

NOTES

NOTES

NOTES

NOTES

NOTES